Zen Philosophy, Zen Practice

Zen Philosophy, Zen Practice

Thich Thien-An, D. Litt.

Co-published by

Dharma Publishing

College of Oriental Studies

International Standard Book Number 0-913546-33-x
Library of Congress Catalogue Card Number: 75-20003

Frontispiece: Śākyamuni Buddha
Photo credits:
Otis Thomas, pages 37, 39, 111
Dennis Broderick, page 146

Typeset in Fototronic Garamond
and printed by Dharma Press
Printed in the United States of America

9

Foreword

Since the eighth century, Zen and Nyingma have shared many similarities in both philosophy and meditation practice. So I am very happy that Dharma Publishing and the College of Oriental Studies can now mutually work together to make available these basic Buddhist teachings.

Proper instructions and guidance are essential to reveal the Buddha nature within us. This Buddha nature is like a raw diamond. The cleaning, cutting and polishing is like the Buddha's methods. By learning to use the proper method at the proper time, we can transform all our difficulties and problems into the means for realizing our Buddha nature.

To receive the teachings we should begin with an open mind and listen carefully, ready to investigate all possibilities. The more we examine, the more we can verify the teachings through our own experience. But self-understanding is not just intellectual. When the teachings are truly understood, there is

little difference between meditation and all other activities.
The teachings and our experience become the same.

The Buddhadharma is open to everyone as it is not separate
from one's own mind. *Zen Philosophy, Zen Practice* will be a
valuable guide for all those who sincerely wish to discover this
mind-nature for themselves.

TARTHANG TULKU

Founder of the Tibetan Nyingma
Meditation Center and the
Nyingma Institute, Berkeley, California

Contents

Preface

In the history of mankind, if there is any time when we should revise the famous saying of Kipling about the East and the West, that time is now. The saying that would result from such a revision might read: "East is East and West is West, and for the peace of mankind and the world both must understand one another." This mutual exchange of understanding is already in progress. While Western civilization and technology are now penetrating the East, at the same time an increasing number of people in the West are beginning to look with interest at the civilization of the East. The focus of this interest is Eastern religion, and especially those techniques of self-awareness and self-realization which form its essence. One of these forms of religious practice is Zen Buddhism, a spiritual discipline which has existed for over a thousand years in the East and which may be taken to represent the apex of Asian spirituality.

The aim of this book is to present the basic teachings and techniques of Zen Buddhism to man in the West. Its approach, however, is not academic and scholastic but practical: to guide the expanding interest of Westerners in Zen Buddhism towards easy understanding and easy practice. The text itself was developed from a series of lectures I gave during 1972 and 1973 at the International Buddhist Meditation Center, the College of Oriental Studies, Graduate School, in Los Angeles and at the University of California in Los Angeles. The original motivation to transcribe and publish these lectures in book form was the request of the Center's members, students and friends who wished to have ready access to them, as well as to make them available to those who had not been able to attend the lectures themselves.

The book consists of fourteen chapters, each of which was first given as a public lecture. Because of this format, general ideas and the basics of understanding are emphasized. Following each lecture is a different method of practice used in Zen Buddhism. The purpose of this added feature is to give each reader the opportunity to fully experience Zen practice for himself and to choose from a variety of methods of practice that technique he finds most effective for himself. The approach to Zen taken in these lectures is non-sectarian. If the three existing Zen schools in Japan and the five branches of Chinese Zen all originate from Hui-Neng, the Sixth Patriarch of Zen Buddhism in China, and if further, the different schools of Buddhism all spring from the Buddha and the Patriarchs, what reason is there to harp on sectarian differences? In my own experience, which includes training in Buddhist monasteries and Zen temples from the time I was fourteen years old, all these different schools, sects and methods lead to the same goal: the discovery of one's true nature, the attainment of

Ven. Dr. Thich Thien-An, Zen Master from Vietnam, is Abbot of the International Buddhist Meditation Center and President of the College of Oriental Studies, Los Angeles. The Master is pictured in the traditional, formal attire of a Great Dharma Master, including the twenty-five fold *keśa* or rice-field robe, the Archbishop's hat, *ojuzu* (prayer beads) and *shakujo*, a staff consisting of six rings looped through a larger ring which is rattled in order to awaken all beings in the six realms to their Buddha nature.

enlightenment and the realization of Nirvāṇa. With this in mind, the different chapters present the various teachings and practices of Zen Buddhism as alternative routes leading to this goal.

Here I would like to express my sincere thanks to Rev. Dr. Bodhi, former lecturer in philosophy at California State University at Fullerton and assistant director of the International Buddhist Meditation Center, for the time he spent correcting the language of these lectures and editing them into their present form. His tremendous background of knowledge and experience in Buddhism has made them more enjoyable and easier to read. I would also like to express my gratitude to my friends Dr. Edward Wortz and Dr. David Nowlis for reading the manuscript and making many valuable suggestions, and to Vimala Nowlis and Cate Mann for the typing and proofreading. In addition, I would like to thank Rev. Karuṇā Dharma, secretary of the College and Meditation Center, for her photography and final editing of the manuscript. Finally, I wish to express my deep thanks to those friends and students of the Meditation Center and of the College who encouraged me in these lectures and suggested their development into book form.

As the title of the work indicates, I hope this book will give newcomers to Zen Buddhism a general overview of the central concepts of Zen philosophy and the rudiments of Zen practice. From this, I hope their interest will grow and their practice deepen so that they may find the true meaning of life and true peace for themselves and others. May all attain the eternal peace—Nirvāṇa.

Thich Thien-An
Los Angeles, Spring 1975

1

The Buddha
and the Origins of Zen

Sometimes people who are new to the study of Zen Buddhism arrive with the idea that Zen and Buddhism are two different things. Some, in fact, even ask what the difference is between Buddhism and Zen. The answer to this question is that Zen and Buddhism are not different. Zen is one method or school of Buddhism, and those who practice according to this method regard it as the very essence of Buddhism. Therefore, when we use the term Buddhism, it is to refer to the religious tradition stemming from the teaching of the Buddha as a whole; when we use the term Zen, it is to refer to a school or method of meditation within that tradition. But we cannot take the Buddhism out of Zen without it ceasing to be Zen, just as we cannot take the chlorine out of salt without it ceasing to be salt. It is also commonly believed that Zen Buddhism is a religious phenomenon peculiar to Japan. This is especially the case with many in the Western world who first learned about Zen through the work of the great Japanese scholar D. T.

Suzuki. But while Zen may truly be the flower of Japanese civilization, the Zen school of Buddhism has not been confined to Japan but has flourished in other countries as well. Its origins go back to India, and to follow its history would lead us through China, Korea and Vietnam. The Japanese word "Zen" is, in fact, a Japanese rendering of the Chinese word "Ch'an," and this in turn is an attempt at a phonetic rendering of the Sanskrit word "Dhyāna," which means meditation or contemplation. In Vietnam we use a similar word "Thien." The pronunciation differs from country to country, but the method is the same: the method of meditation and contemplation, the method of keeping the mind calm and quiet, the method of self-realization and discovering that the true nature is, in fact, nothing less than the Buddha nature.

Some may ask who is the founder of Zen Buddhism. When we seek for the founder of Zen Buddhism, we must go back a long way, past the Japanese Zen masters, the Chinese Ch'an masters and the patriarchs, even past Bodhidharma, right back to the Buddha himself. The founder of Buddhism and the founder of Zen Buddhism are one and the same, for the fountainhead of both is the enlightenment experience of the Buddha. Therefore, we would like to introduce Zen Buddhism by speaking a little about the Buddha, his life, his character and his accomplishments. Much has already been written about the biographical details of the Buddha's life, so we will not deal with these so much as with the significance of that life for our own present-day world.

The word "Buddha" is not a proper name but a title meaning "Enlightened One" or "Awakened One." The man who was to be called the Buddha was not born enlightened, but like us, unenlightened; it was only later, after his Enlightenment, that he came to be called Śākyamuni Buddha, the Enlightened One of the Śākya clan. His given name was

Siddhartha Gautama, and he was born a prince, the son of a king in the northeastern part of India. Though he was destined to become ruler of that kingdom himself, as he reached maturity the young prince grew disillusioned with his lot. For he saw that all living beings were subject to suffering—to the suffering of birth, sickness, old age and death—and moved by compassion, he wished to be able to relieve their suffering. In his moments of deep reflection he thought: "If I continue as a prince and become king in the future, I may be able to win some measure of happiness for myself and for those around me. But how can I help all beings find happiness? How can I save all beings from suffering? There must be a way, and I am determined to find it." So thinking, he left his palace, wandered beyond the farthest bounds of his kingdom and went deep into the mountains seeking the way to deliverance from suffering, not for himself alone but for all beings.

Such a move on the part of the prince was not easy. It called for great courage and adamantine determination to renounce his right to the throne, to give up everything in order to roam in the forest clothed in rags, feeding on alms and meditating without cessation. It may not be so difficult for some of us to give up a little ease and comfort to practice Zen, or even to leave home to become a Zen monk or nun. But for a man in a high position, such as a king or prince or president or governor, to give up everything for the unknown in order to seek the happiness and welfare of others—that is not easy at all. Perhaps it is the most difficult task in the world. But this is what the young prince Siddhartha did. He left behind his wife, his child and his wealth, renounced all the promised power and glory that were to be his in order to meditate in solitude far from the haunts of men. We may at this point ask: "Why should he do that?" The answer is: his great compassion. What led him to make such sacrifices time and time again was his

great compassion, his boundless sympathy with the sufferings
of others and his determination to find a way out of suffering
that all could tread. It is, above all, for his great compassion that
we love and admire the Buddha, for it was this compassion that
stood behind all his sacrifices and all his achievements.

After leaving his palace, the future Buddha sought out
famous yoga masters for instruction and practiced with great
vigor the forms of yoga meditation they taught him. But
though he practiced very hard, still he did not succeed in
finding the higher realization he was searching for, the realization of Nirvāṇa. He achieved many lofty spiritual states,
states of consciousness far beyond the limits ordinarily known
to men. But he realized that they were not yet the ultimate,
that however exalted they may have been, they still fell short of
the highest goal: Enlightenment and Nirvāṇa. So he turned to
another method popular among truth-seekers in ancient India,
the method of extreme asceticism and self-mortification. For
six years he starved and tortured his mind and body, but these
practices brought him not to peace, but to the edge of death.

Then one day he thought to himself: "For the last six years
I have practiced yoga meditation and asceticism, seeking the
truth outside myself. But I have failed and have not obtained
the goal. Maybe that goal, that reality, Nirvāṇa, is not outside
but inside." Accordingly, he gave up the search for Nirvāṇa
as something to be obtained from outside and turned his
contemplation within, seeking the truth in himself. He left his
yoga teachers and ascetic friends, went off by himself, sat
beneath a tree and began practicing meditation in a new way,
"not seeking truth from the outside but inside." So strong was
his determination that he vowed: "If I do not succeed in this
way, I will not get up from this place." He practiced this
inward way for forty-nine days until suddenly he experienced

enlightenment and became the Buddha, the Enlightened One. By turning inward upon himself, he discovered his true nature, or Buddha nature, and became a Buddha. This marked the origin of Zen Buddhism.

The distinctive feature of the Buddha's practice at the time of his enlightenment was his inner search. This is the method of Zen Buddhism and indicates just where it differs from other religions and spiritual practices. Most other religions place a supreme God above man and then ask that he pray to God and worship him, implying that reality is to be sought externally. The way of Zen is very different, for Zen holds that reality is to be gotten hold of, not externally, but inwardly. The truth is to be found in our own nature and nowhere else. Every living being has within himself the Buddha nature, the principle of enlightenment. To become a Buddha is simply to discover this Buddha nature, always present within, eternally shining. It is like the moon and sun. The moon and sun continually shine and give forth light, but when the clouds cover them, we cannot see the moonlight or sunshine. The goal is to eliminate the clouds, for when they fly away, we can once again see the light. In the same way, we always have within ourselves the nature of Buddha, but when our desires and attachments cover it up, it does not appear. Because our minds are constantly occupied with wayward thoughts—thoughts of worry and of happiness, of hatred and anger, of friend and foe—we cannot discover the Buddha nature within. But when we do discover it, it is not new at all. When this happens, then there is no difference between us and the Buddha. The Buddha was not a god or any kind of supernatural being. Like us, he was born a man. The difference between the Buddha and an ordinary man is simply that the former has awakened to his Buddha nature while the latter is still deluded about it. However, whether we are awakened or deluded, the Buddha nature is equally present in all beings, and therefore beings even in the thickest state of delusion still have the potential to become Buddhas.

Because all beings have the potential to become enlightened, they may be considered as future Buddhas and, in their deepest nature, as Buddhas already. Therefore, when we greet each other in a Buddhist temple or Zen monastery, we do not shake hands, but join our palms together to pay respect to each other. Why do we do this? We do this because the people we meet are potential Buddhas. Spiritually, beneath the outward differences of color, race, sex or nationality, everybody is equal, for everybody has the Buddha nature. When he attained enlightenment, the Buddha realized that the Buddha nature is equally present in all living beings. Thus he taught throughout his life that all beings are fundamentally the same and should be treated equally without discrimination. He opposed the caste-system which prevailed in the Indian society of his day, which divided men into rigid groups on the basis of artificial distinctions. He taught that, "Just as the waters of the great rivers, on reaching the mighty ocean, abandon their former names and go by the name of just 'ocean', so men of the four castes—the nobles, brahmins, the merchants and the serfs—on joining the Buddhist community, abandon their former lineage and become known as just Buddhists." Against this oppressive caste-system, the Buddha proclaimed the equality of men—the equality between man and man, and also between man and Buddha.

We all work very hard each day. Some seek money, others seek fame, still others seek power and pleasure and luxury. But though we fill our day with labor and toil, seldom do we do any work on ourselves. It is only at rare intervals that we turn from our concern with the outside world to reflect upon the light of awareness inwardly. By practicing Zen we seek to turn within and discover our true nature. We do not look above, we do not look below, we do not look to the east or west or to the north or south; we look into ourselves, for within ourselves and there alone is the center upon which the whole universe turns. This is the way of Zen first proclaimed by Śākyamuni Buddha more than 2500 years ago.

But the Zen method of self-analysis, self-reflection and self-discovery should never be taken to imply that we are to shut ourselves off from communion with our fellow men. To follow the way of Zen is not to become isolated in a cage or cell, but to become free and open in our relations with our fellow beings. The search for self-realization always has as its counterpart the development of a new way of relating to others, a way imbued with compassion, love and sympathy with all that live. And the attainment of self-realization always has as its outcome the spontaneous flowering of this new attitude. Thus we see in the life of Śākyamuni Buddha that before his Enlightenment he vowed to deliver all sentient beings from suffering; and after his Enlightenment, he did not keep his realization to himself, but for forty-nine years walked the dusty roads of India proclaiming his doctrine, the Dharma, founding the Saṅgha, or brotherhood of monks, and working very hard to teach and transform living beings.

Compassion and loving-kindness are of the utmost importance for men, for despite our strivings towards self-sufficiency, it remains a fact that men need one another. No man is an island. An island can exist alone in the sea, but a man cannot live alone. We need each other, and we must come to regard one another as friends and helpers whom we can look toward for mutual support. All men, as the doctrine of rebirth implies, are really brothers to each other, literally members of the same family, for in the repeated round of rebirth there is not one man or woman who has not at some time in the past been our

The Bodhisattva Kwan-Yin represents compassion and the salvation of all living beings. The lotus flowers, one on which she stands and the other which she holds, symbolize purity, which can be found even in the world of Saṃsāra.

father or mother, our sister or brother. Therefore we must learn to love each other, to respect each other, to protect each other and to give to the other what we would have for ourselves. To practice Zen Buddhism is to train oneself to eliminate hatred, anger and selfishness and to develop loving-kindness towards all. We have our physical bodies and our own lives, but still we can live in harmony with each other and help each other to the best of our ability. If we are not happy when we see others, they will also feel unhappy, but if we are happy, they will share that happiness with us.

Our lives are inseparably linked together. Whatever we do affects others and rebounds upon ourselves. Love evokes love, hatred evokes hatred. Therefore an ancient Buddhist text says: "Hatred does not cease by hatred, hatred ceases only by love." This means that we cannot use hatred to stop hatred; we must use love. We cannot use war to stop war; we must use love and mutual respect. For it is only love, silent and patient love, that can open the gates to peace.

By its spirit of love and universal compassion, Buddhism spread peacefully from its original home in India to diverse parts of the world. In Buddhism there are two traditional schools, the Theravāda (or Hīnayāna) and the Mahāyāna. Theravāda Buddhism flourishes in Ceylon, Burma, Thailand, Laos and Cambodia—the countries of Southeast Asia. The other tradition, known as Mahāyāna Buddhism, has been practiced in Tibet, China, Japan, Korea, Mongolia and Vietnam.

In the present century Buddhism has spread from Asia to the Western world, including the United States, where many have begun to study and practice its teachings. The Buddhist school that has proved most attractive thus far to Western man is Zen Buddhism, which belongs to the Mahāyāna tradition of Buddhism. Why is this? Primarily because Western man has seen the great practical value of Zen Buddhism, the great contribution the Zen method can make to his daily life. Western man is always busy, always active, his whole attention riveted outward upon the task of conquering and mastering the external world. Zen meditation helps him free his mind from this excessive occupation with outward things and lets him enjoy the true rest and quiet that comes from within.

Another reason why Zen appeals to Western man lies, perhaps, in the challenge it presents to his intellect, a challenge which invites further investigation and actual practice. Western man is very intellectual, and Zen presents a philosophy profound enough to meet the demands of his intellect. Man tends by nature to be lazy. Most people would rather go to church to pray to some supreme being for salvation than work out their salvation by themselves. But Zen does not allow such a shrugging off of the work: it demands that its followers think. We ask: "What am I? What is the meaning of life? What is the purpose of life? What is my true self?" Zen does not give us ready-made answers to these questions, but it shows us the method by which we can answer these questions for ourselves: the method of meditation.

Up to now, many people in the West have tended to misunderstand the meaning of practicing meditation. Perhaps when some of our friends see us sitting in meditation, they ask us why we are wasting our time. To them meditation is meaningless. But to us who practice meditation, it is an essential and very meaningful part of our lives. All day long, every day of the week, every week of the month, every month of the year, we work at our business or occupation. To give balance to our lives it is necessary to sit quietly, to learn to accept and experience rather than to control, to look within rather than without. When we work during the daytime, we usually do not work for an inner goal but for something external to ourselves. We work because we want money, and we want money because we want a better and more comfortable life. But when we sit in meditation, it is not for any material goal, but to realize the true meaning of life—to discover our true self. What is the true self? What is the purpose of life? These questions require intelligent understanding. Therefore, most of the people who come to Zen Buddhism are intelligent, not necessarily in the sense that they hold a high degree, but in the sense that they are able and willing to do the kind of intellectual and spiritual work that Zen demands from those who would follow its way. For the way of Zen is not the way of prayer and worship but the way of meditation. This is something we have to practice ourselves; there is nobody that can do the work for us.

Why do we have to meditate? According to Buddhism, our mind behaves like a monkey, restless and always jumping; it is therefore called a "monkey-mind." Through meditation we try to keep that monkey-mind still, to keep it calm and quiet and pure. When our mind is still, we realize that the Buddha is inside us, that the whole universe is inside us and that our true nature is one with the Buddha nature. So the most important task is to keep our minds quiet, a task which may be simple to understand but is not simple to practice. Yet practice is all important; knowing by itself is nothing—doing is of more value. The method of Zen is the scientific method: we learn by doing, by our own experience.

METHOD OF PRACTICE

To fully experience the benefit of meditation it is best to practice in a quiet place with a congenial atmosphere, such as a meditation center or in a quiet, secluded area of the home. The quality of meditation is strongly influenced by the environment. While meditating, it is best to have a soft light or candles, incense burning, and some fresh flowers tastefully arranged about a small altar.

The first thing to learn in practicing meditation is the proper posture. Strictly speaking, Zen meditation has nothing to do with any particular posture. At its highest level, meditation is to be practiced in the midst of all sorts of activities—standing, walking, studying, working, driving, etc. In the history of Zen Buddhism many a master attained enlightenment while washing dishes, cooking, carrying water and collecting fuel. So when it is our turn to wash dishes, we should not complain. If the mind is kept under control and the adept remains mindful of what he is doing, even washing dishes can become a vehicle to self-realization.

However, while we can meditate in any activity, the best way to control the mind is by the practice of sitting meditation. In the Zen tradition there are two ways of sitting, the full-lotus and the half-lotus. The full-lotus posture involves placing each foot across the opposite thigh. The half-lotus involves placing one foot across the opposite thigh with the other foot resting upon the ground. If the half-lotus is too difficult, the beginner may move his foot from his thigh, placing it directly on the floor in front of the other leg, the ankles close together. The knees should be spread as far apart as possible, resting on the floor. Higher cushions will help to lower the knees to the proper position. If the meditator cannot sit on the floor, a chair may be used. The most important point in sitting is to hold the body erect, stable and comfortable. The meditator must not let the body lean to the right or left, forward or backward, but he must keep it straight. When the body is stabilized through the proper posture, the mind too becomes stable and calm, and with a calm mind the practice of mental concentration can be undertaken.

Once the body is erect, the hands are placed on the lap, the left hand on the right palm; both hands rest near the lower abdomen. The two thumbs should be joined at the top, making an empty circle. This circle represents the moon, the symbol of emptiness, *mu*. The circle signifies that during meditation while the hands are empty, the mind is also empty. Nothing is held in the hands, nothing is held in the mind. The mind is kept empty. A meditator does not think about the past and the future, does not worry about the external world, but

Members of an advanced Zen class, assuming the traditional formal posture, begin daily practice.

just sits in meditation, at one with himself here and now. If meditating alone, the eyes may be kept partially open, looking downwards at a distance of about three feet. If practice is with a group, it is best to close the eyes to avoid distraction. The tongue should be touching the upper part of the mouth to avoid excessive salivation.

The most important thing in meditation is to keep the mind under control, so it can return to its natural condition of calm and quiet. To regulate the mind, the first and most effective method is awareness of breathing. Breathing in the Zen tradition differs from yogic breathing, where the meditator breathes deeply and retains the air for long periods of time. In Zen everything is natural. The sitter just breathes in and out lightly and naturally, but remains aware of his breathing. He does not allow his mind to wander here and there. He ties it down to the here and now of present existence. When he finishes one cycle of inhalation and exhalation, as he finishes breathing out he counts one; when he finishes the second cycle, he counts two; and so on, up to ten. Then he counts backwards from ten down to one. This method is very simple, but it is not easy to practice. As we practice, many times we will find that the mind is drifting away from its object. We may find ourselves counting: "One, what time is it? Two, what am I going to do tomorrow? Three, what is the best way to go home tonight? etc." When the mind drifts, the sitter should just let go of all extraneous thoughts and bring his attention back to the breathing, just breathing in and out fully aware of what he is doing. Just counting and breathing—there is nothing more.

2

Bodhidharma: The Patriarch from the West

When looking into the origins of Zen Buddhism, we find that the real founder of Zen is none other than the Buddha himself. Through the practice of inward meditation the Buddha attained Supreme Enlightenment and thereby became the Awakened One, the Lord of Wisdom and Compassion. For forty-nine years following his Enlightenment, the Buddha wandered across the subcontinent of India, proclaiming the doctrine and teaching the way to deliverance until, at the ripe age of eighty, he entered Parinirvāṇa, surrounded by his many disciples. After the Parinirvāṇa, or passing away, of the Buddha, the transmission of his teaching moved in two different directions. One line of transmission developed into what is called Theravāda or Hīnayāna Buddhism and travelled southward to Ceylon, Burma, Thailand, Cambodia and Laos. The other developed into what is called Mahāyāna Buddhism and travelled northward to Tibet, Nepal, Mongolia, China, Japan, Korea and Vietnam.

Zen Buddhism is one of the most important sects of
Mahāyāna Buddhism. To be sure, Zen did not exist as a
separate sect in India, but the essential element was there: the
practice of meditation as a way to enlightenment, i.e., to the
realization of one's true nature. This transmission of enlightenment went directly back to the Buddha. In the forty-nine
years of his ministry, the Buddha enlightened many people
and had many distinguished disciples. Shortly before entering
into Parinirvāṇa, he transmitted his Mind-Seal, the certification
of enlightenment, to Mahākāśyapa, who thereby became the
First Patriarch of Buddhism in general, and of Zen Buddhism
in particular. Mahākāśyapa, in turn, before his own passing,
transmitted the Mind-Seal to Ānanda, who himself passed
it on to his own chief disciple. Thus, in this way, the Mind
of Enlightenment was transmitted from master to disciple,
generation after generation, through twenty-eight Indian
patriarchs. Then, in the sixth century A.D., the transmission
underwent a new turn: the Mind-Seal was carried from India
to China. The figure responsible for bringing the Mind-
Doctrine to China was an Indian master named Bodhidharma,
the Twenty-eighth Patriarch of Buddhism in India and the First
Patriarch of Zen Buddhism in China. It is to Bodhidharma and
his message that we turn next.

Buddhism began to spread to the countries neighboring
India at an early time. In the third century B.C., Buddhist
missionaries brought the Buddha's teachings to Ceylon, and
from the beginning of the Christian era onwards, Buddhist
monks began to propagate Buddhism in China. Thus, when
Bodhidharma arrived in China in 520 A.D., Buddhism was
already well established. The scriptures were studied, Buddha-
images created, and monasteries built. The temples were well
attended. Numbers of Chinese men and women became
monks and nuns, and many people earnestly practiced the

Buddha's teaching in their daily life. Well then, one might ask, if this was the case, what need was there for Bodhidharma to go to China? What did he have to give the Chinese that they did not have already? Bodhidharma had something very special to give the Chinese. It was not at all like the things the other Buddhist missionaries brought to China. It was not an image, a book, a rosary, a robe or a mantra. It could not be touched with the hands, seen by the eyes, tasted by the mouth or heard by the ears. In fact, when Bodhidharma arrived in China, he was completely empty-handed. Now one might think, "Ah, then he must have brought nothing." This may be right, but if he brought nothing, it was a very special "nothing." This "nothing" was a message, a message which went thus:

> A special transmission outside the scriptures;
> No dependence upon words and letters;
> Direct pointing at the mind of man;
> Seeing into one's nature and the attainment of Buddhahood.

In this message is contained the whole basic philosophy of Zen Buddhism. Bodhidharma's mission to China and the "nothing" he brought, transformed the Far East.

Bodhidharma came to China about 520 A.D., a thousand years after the time of the Buddha. When he arrived, Buddhism was well established. There were many sincere Chinese Buddhists who understood the doctrine well, generously supported the religion and cultivated the way with great energy. Nevertheless, something was lacking. What was lacking was the transmission of the Mind of Enlightenment, the patriarchal Mind-Seal originally passed from the Buddha to Mahākāśyapa. It was this transmission that Bodhidharma came to deliver to China.

At the time of his arrival, the ruler of China was Emperor Wu-Ti of the Liang dynasty. Emperor Wu-Ti was an ardent

Buddhist, a scholar as well as a supporter and devotee. Through his contacts with other Buddhist masters, he had come to understand Buddhist philosophy very well. When he heard that the great master Bodhidharma had arrived in China, he was beside himself with delight and promptly invited the master to his court. The opportunity to see and learn from such a master was all too rare! When Bodhidharma entered the court, the Emperor, after paying his proper respects, spoke to the Master thus: "For a long time I have used my own money to support many Buddhist temples and ordain many Buddhist monks and nuns. I have built schools for children and hospitals for the sick and aged. I have printed many Buddhist texts for free distribution to the people. I have done so many good things for Buddhism and for my people. Would you please tell me how much merit I will get?" Without a moment's hesitation Bodhidharma answered: "No merit at all." The response struck the Emperor like a slap. The other masters had all taught him quite differently. "Do good," they said, "and you will receive good; do bad and you will receive bad. Effects follow causes as shadows follow figures." But now the Emperor thought, "Though I have done many good things, this master says 'no merit at all.' " He was perplexed.

Why did Bodhidharma answer the way he did? Perhaps he wanted to say that if we do good with the desire to gain merits for ourselves, that is not good. We are not working for the welfare of others, we are not working to promote the Dharma; we are working for our own welfare, we are working to promote ourselves. We might get some worldly merit, but how can we gain any supramundane merit, merit for Enlightenment or Nirvāṇa? Perhaps this is what Bodhidharma meant to say, but Bodhidharma was not the kind of man to give long explanations. Therefore, without a moment's hesitation he answered: "No merit at all."

This water color of Bodhidharma, painted by Prof. Ashikaga, former chairman of the Dept. of Oriental Languages, U. of California at Los Angeles, was presented to the author when he served as a visiting professor in 1966. It now hangs in the zendo of the International Buddhist Meditation Center.

The Emperor then asked Bodhidharma another question: "Would you please tell me, what is the essence of Buddhism?" Short and sharp the answer came: "No essence at all." The Emperor was stunned. No essence at all? When he had asked the other masters this question, they explained, with many words, arguments, illustrations and proofs, the basic doctrines of Buddhism. One showed that the doctrine of cause and effect is the essence of Buddhism, another the theory of karma and rebirth, another the Four Noble Truths, the Eightfold Noble Path, the Bodhisattva ideal, etc. But here is this great, highly-respected master, and he answers, "No essence at all." Had he travelled all the way from India to China merely to say this?

Could this be the meaning of the Patriarch's coming from the West?

Why did Bodhidharma answer the way he did? Perhaps he wanted to say that all the teachings in Buddhism are but methods to be practiced, skillful means or expedients, and that what constitutes the essence for one man may not be the essence for another. Perhaps he wanted to say that all phenomena are conditioned, relative and void, and therefore contain no essence at all. Or perhaps he wanted to say that the original Mind of Enlightenment is the All-Illumining Void in which there is nothing to be grasped and no one to grasp, and therefore no essence at all. But Bodhidharma was not the kind of man to waste words. Therefore, short and sharp the answer came: "No essence at all."

This answer did not please the Emperor. However, he tried to be patient and asked one more question of Bodhidharma: "You say that, according to Buddhism, everything is nothing, that all things have no essence. Well then, who is he that is talking with me now?" "I do not know." This reply shocked the Emperor. He lost his patience, dismissed Bodhidharma from his court and retired to his chambers, his head swirling in confusion.

Meanwhile, left to himself, Bodhidharma thought: "This man is a Buddhist scholar, and yet even he could not understand. Perhaps conditions are not yet favorable enough for me to teach." So he went to the Shao-Lin monastery in the state of Wei, sat cross-legged before a wall and entered into a deep state of meditation. He sat like this for nine years, waiting for conditions to ripen, waiting for someone to appear who would be capable of receiving the transmission of the wonderful Buddha Mind, that priceless treasure he had travelled all the way from India to China to transmit.

For nine years he sat in meditation facing the wall, practicing *pi-kuan*, or "wall-contemplation." He never talked to anyone; he just sat. Then one day a Chinese monk named Shen-Kuang (Hui-Ke) approached him and asked for instruction. Bodhidharma remained silent. A second and third time the monk asked, a second and third time Bodhidharma remained silent. Again and again the monk begged to be taught, but still the Master did not budge. Finally, seeing the sincerity of the monk, he realized that here was a man capable of receiving the Dharma. He turned to him and said: "What do you want from me?" Kuang replied: "For a long time I have tried to keep my mind calm and pure by practicing meditation. But when I meditate, I become bothered by many thoughts and cannot keep my mind calm. Would you please tell me how to pacify my mind?" Bodhidharma smiled and answered: "Bring me that mind, and I will help you pacify it." Kuang stopped, searched within looking for his mind, and after a time said: "I am looking for my mind, but I cannot find it." "There," Bodhidharma declared, "I have already pacified it!" With these words, Kuang's mad mind suddenly halted. A veil lifted. He was enlightened. When he took the mind to be real, then the wandering mind disturbed him in his meditation. But now that he could not find that wandering mind, he realized the mind is no-mind, that nothing can be disturbed. And from that no-mind he realized the One-Mind. From that time on Shen-Kuang became the disciple of Bodhidharma and received the Buddhist name Hui-Ke. After Bodhidharma's passing, Hui-Ke inherited the robe and bowl and became the Second Patriarch of Chinese Zen Buddhism.

The entirety of Zen philosophy lies in the special message that Bodhidharma brought from India to China. The first two lines are: "A special transmission outside the scriptures; No dependence upon words and letters." These lines point to the difference between Zen Buddhism and the other schools of

Buddhism, as well as between Zen and other religions. All other religions and Buddhist schools trace their teaching to particular scriptures which they regard as the supreme authority in the sphere of truth. From generation to generation these scriptures are read, studied and chanted. In Zen Buddhism, however, there are no such scriptures. Special words and letters count for nothing. Why? Because understanding Zen is not a matter of book learning, but of personal experience.

One may ask, "In Zen are not some of the sutras read and studied, such as the *Diamond Sūtra* and the *Laṅkāvatāra Sūtra*? And do they not chant the *Heart Sūtra* every day in Zen monasteries all around the world?" The answer to these questions is yes, but in Zen the scriptures play a different role than they do in other religions. For Zen the sutras are not the truth, but only guides to the truth. We regard the Buddha's teaching as a finger pointing to the moon. The truth, or Nirvāṇa, is the moon; the Buddha's teaching is the finger. We only use the finger as a guide to find the direction of the moon. But the finger is too short to reach the moon. If we wish to see the moon, what must we do? We leave the finger behind and look directly at the moon. And once the moon is seen, the finger is no longer needed. The same principle applies to the role of the Buddha's teaching in Zen Buddhism. The scriptures only point out the direction of the truth, but once we know the direction we have to leave the scriptures behind and experience the truth for ourselves. The scriptures are no substitute for our own experience. They are of value insofar as they give us a notion of what the truth is like and of where it is to be found. But once we know the direction, we have to leave all letters and words behind. We have to transcend even the word of the Buddha, for when we cling to it, it becomes an obstacle to enlightenment rather than a guide. In Zen Buddhism experience counts for everything. And to achieve experience, that is,

During Sunday morning service and lecture, the Ven. Master Thich Thien-An reminds followers never to mistake the finger for the moon.

to attain enlightenment and realize Nirvāṇa, practice is necessary. We cannot get anywhere without practice.

This is the meaning of the first two lines of Bodhidharma's message. The next two lines read: "Direct pointing at the mind of man; Seeing into one's nature and the attainment of Buddhahood." These two lines show us the method of Zen Buddhism.

The way of Zen does not involve worshipping or praying to some supernatural being, but seeing into our true nature and realizing that our true nature is Buddha nature. To arrive at this insight we must cultivate ourselves; we must practice. How can we discover our true nature if we blindly cling to the scriptures and do not practice for ourselves? If we go to a Zen center and speak with a Zen master, sometimes he may answer our questions with silence. This is the silence of knowledge. It does not mean that the Zen master does not know how to answer; rather, it means that he is trying to communicate that there are some things which cannot be explained in words, things which will ever remain in the dark until we discover them through our own experience.

Our language is limited. It can be used only to express limited truths. To express ultimate truth—Nirvāṇa—many words may be used, but none are adequate. If we wish to understand, we must experience, and to experience we must practice. There is no other way. Suppose we hold a cup of tea in our hand. We take a sip and say: "This is good tea." If another has not tasted the tea himself, he may believe us, but still he does not know that the tea is good. If he wants to know how good the tea is, he must taste it himself. Then he will know how good it is. Similarly with the Buddha's teaching. We may accept it, believe it and study it, but unless we practice and realize the teaching for ourselves, we cannot say that we know it.

Learning Zen is also like learning how to swim. When a person goes to a swimming class, the instructor will show him some basic methods and techniques, and then the rest is up to him. If he does not jump into the water and try to swim, he will never be a swimmer. The only way to learn is to jump into the water and begin practicing what the instructor taught. And if he practices hard enough, he may become a good swimmer.

In Zen Buddhism it is the same way. If we want to become enlightened, we must go to a teacher and receive some instructions. But once we receive instructions, the most important thing is to put them into practice. Only through practice can we hope to achieve enlightenment.

In the last two lines of Bodhidharma's message we also find the recognition that everybody has a Buddha nature. We all are potential Buddhas. But why are we not Buddhas, in fact? We are not Buddhas because our minds are full of worries, desires, attachments and selfishness. If we want to discover our Buddha nature and become Buddhas, we must learn to keep our minds calm and pure; then we can accomplish the Buddha way. Zen gives us the method to discover our Buddha nature. Through meditation we learn to keep our minds calm and quiet, and when our minds are calm and quiet, then we can see our pure mind, discover our true nature and attain Buddhahood. The Buddha and the whole universe are present in the quiet mind. We cannot find them by looking outside, but only within. To discover our true nature is the highest realization, and this realization can take place in the present life. There is no need to wait until we die to obtain the ultimate. In Christianity the belief is that if a man is good now, when he dies his soul will go to heaven and enjoy happiness there. But according to Zen, Nirvāṇa is to be achieved not only after death, but here and now. For what is Nirvāṇa? Nirvāṇa is a state of mind. When the mind is enlightened, we can experience the bliss of Nirvāṇa wherever we are, at any time. Consider the Buddha: did he not experience Nirvāṇa during his lifetime? And yet his fellow countrymen were not in Nirvāṇa. To the Buddha, everything in this world is Nirvāṇa, everything is perfect. When the mind is changed from ignorance to enlightenment, Saṃsāra is transformed into Nirvāṇa. When we are enlightened, we realize that the Buddha and everything are one: that is Suchness,

Oneness, or Tathatā. To realize the oneness of everything is *kensho*, "seeing into one's nature." The non-discriminating mind has no distinctions between subject and object, high and low, good and bad, the Buddha and oneself, Saṃsāra and Nirvāṇa. In Zen Buddhism *kensho* is usually considered the first step on the path of Enlightenment, but it is perhaps the most important step because it opens the mind's eye to a new dimension of existence and gives us a direct experience of oneness with the universe.

The message Bodhidharma brought to China was the method of meditation for the purpose of achieving enlightenment or self-realization. He taught that meditation practice must be fused with daily life. It is best to devote ten or twenty minutes after waking in the morning to the practice of meditation, and again ten or twenty minutes before retiring at night. It is true that sitting in meditation may not be the only way to obtain self-realization, but without the discipline of daily meditation it is very difficult to become enlightened.

METHOD OF PRACTICE

After some meditation experience in the breathing process described in chapter one, the student may introduce a variation into his practice. After assuming the correct bodily posture for meditation, the mind settles into a quiet state, the meditator begins to breathe lightly, softly and naturally, counting the breaths from one to ten and from ten to one. During meditation the eyes are closed lightly, but the mind's eye tries to visualize the breath going in and out. Nothing else is seen but the breath, nothing else is thought of but the breath. The meditator must visualize the breaths as clearly as possible. Such practice intensifies the meditation experience and helps to cut discrimination.

3

The Working Meditation of Hui-Neng

When Bodhidharma arrived in China, he brought with him a special message. This message announced the possibility of an immediate experience of enlightenment and the direct attainment of Buddhahood. Bodhidharma also brought with him as an essential part of his message the method leading to enlightenment, the method of inward meditation epitomized by his own nine-year practice of wall-contemplation (*pi-kuan*). By turning the light of awareness back upon itself, it was possible for him to break through the shell of delusions and passions and arrive at an intuitive realization of his true nature.

Bodhidharma's practice of wall-contemplation set the precedent for the development of Zen meditation in the centuries following his arrival. From Śākyamuni Buddha, through Mahākāśyapa and the whole line of Indian patriarchs culminating in Bodhidharma, the essential mode of practice for the attainment of enlightenment was sitting meditation. Bodhidharma carried this method to China, and the early patriarchs of Chinese Zen followed suit. The Second Patriarch, Hui-Ke (468–543), the Third, Seng-Tsan (d. 606), the Fourth, Tao-Hsin (580–651), and the Fifth, Hung-Jen (601–675), all continued the emphasis on sitting meditation.

In time, however, the situation was to change. With the growing interest in Zen Buddhism in China, more and more Chinese people came to the monasteries to study and to practice meditation. Therefore, large monasteries grew up capable of housing and sustaining many people. The Fifth Patriarch Hung-Jen had more than five hundred disciples studying with him, living together in the same monastery. But if all these people were to practice sitting meditation all day, every day, what would happen? Who would clean the rooms? Who would trim the garden? Who would carry water? Who would cook? If these tasks were not performed, the monastery would fall into a state of disorder. Therefore, the Fifth Patriarch introduced a new element into the practice of meditation: meditation was to be performed not only when sitting in quietude, but when actively engaged in the tasks of everyday life as well. This would be a meditation in action, an extension of the principles of inward contemplation into the chores and routines of day to day existence.

In applying this philosophy, the Fifth Patriarch and his disciples worked very hard every day. They would wake up early in the morning, chant sutras and sit in meditation for several hours; then, after a light breakfast, they would disperse to the several sections of the monastery to do what had to be done. Some would go to the garden to look after the vegetables; others would go to the rice fields to tend the rice. Some would sweep and clean the inside of the monastery, while still others would work in the kitchen preparing meals. After work, the monks would go to class for study or read in their rooms or chant sutras, pray, make confession, etc., before the Buddha altar. But the activities of work and study were not to be done casually with a distracted mind; they were to be done mindfully, as an exercise in meditation. Thus the sitting and working aspects of daily life were fused together into a continuum of meditation which lasted from the crack of dawn to the last gong at night signaling the time for sleep.

When the Fifth Patriarch grew old, he realized that the time had come to choose a successor. It had been an established part of the Zen lineage from the time when Sākyamuni Buddha first transmitted the Mind-Seal to Mahākāśyapa for each patriarch to appoint one of his disciples to become his successor and thereby continue the transmission of the patriarchal line. The robe and bowl of patriarchal authority were not to be passed indiscriminately to any disciple, however, nor even to a disciple who shined with intellectual brilliance. They were to be passed only to the disciple who had achieved the deepest spiritual realization, who had fathomed the mind of his master and was thus capable of transmitting enlightenment to others. Each patriarch was thus a member of the spiritual dynasty of the Buddha. So, one day the Fifth Patriarch gathered his many disciples before him in the lecture hall and said: "The question of birth and death is a great affair. Go now and seek for the transcendental wisdom that is within your own minds, and write me a poem about it. He who shows that he has realized his Mind-Essence will be appointed the Sixth Patriarch."

All the disciples withdrew, but all believed that the patriarchship would go automatically to the head monk, Shen-Hsiu, renowned for his great intellect and practice of the Dharma, so no one wrote a poem. Realizing that the burden

was upon him, Shen-Hsiu wrote and submitted to the Patriarch a poem in which he expressed his understanding of Zen.
The poem went like this:

> The body is the Bodhi-tree,
> The mind is like a mirror bright.
> Take heed to keep it always clean,
> And let not dust collect on it.

The first line states that the body is like the Bodhi tree under which the Buddha became enlightened. The body, therefore,
is the foundation for practice, the necessary basis for reaching enlightenment. The second line compares the mind to a
bright mirror, because in its essential nature the mind is the clear
and bright mirror-wisdom of Buddhahood. But our mind in its
usual condition is not yet bright; therefore we must keep it
clean, we must prevent the dust from collecting on it. This is
indicated by the third and fourth lines. The way to cleanse the
mind is by meditation. Through meditation the dust of worldly
desire and attachment is removed from the mind, and the
bright wisdom of the Buddha nature manifests.

After Shen-Hsiu presented his poem to the Patriarch, everybody was very impressed with it. All admired Shen-Hsiu and
had no doubt that he would receive the transmission—all, that
is, except one uneducated monk who worked in the kitchen.
This monk, whose name was Hui-Neng, had recently arrived in
the monastery from the south of China. Upon his arrival the
Fifth Patriarch had assigned him to the lowest type of kitchen
duty, the usual work for newcomers, where he had inconspicu-
ously remained. But now this Hui-Neng not only questioned
the wisdom of the head monk, Shen-Hsiu, but, moreover,
wanted to submit a poem himself. However, Hui-Neng did not
know how to write; therefore he asked a friend to write down
his poem for him and submitted it to the Master. The poem
read:

The Bodhi is not like the tree,
The mirror bright is nowhere shining.
As there is nothing from the first,
Where can the dust itself collect?

As you can see, the meaning of this poem is the exact opposite of Shen-Hsiu's. Where Shen-Hsiu says the body is like the Bodhi tree, Hui-Neng says the Bodhi is not like a tree. Where Shen-Hsiu says the mind is like a miror bright, Hui-Neng says the mirror bright is nowhere shining. And where Shen-Hsiu speaks about dust collecting, Hui-Neng says that there is no dust and nowhere for it to collect.

Hui-Neng's poem is not at all obvious to intellectual understanding, for it is the product of a profound spiritual experience. The poem shows that Hui-Neng had come to the realization that everything in the phenomenal universe is a part of the Dharma-nature, a part of the Dharmakāya, or absolute Body of the Buddha. The Dharma-nature is clean, pure and perfect. It contains no darkness and is always shining, like a jewel. But if the Dharma-nature is always shining everywhere, then where can it not be shining? It is false to look some place specific to see it shine, for it is shining everywhere, illuminating the whole universe. If this is so, then of what use is a bright mirror? In the second two lines Hui-Neng shows his understanding of emptiness (*śūnyatā*) or nothingness (Jap.: *mu*). Why is everything nothing? Because everything is a combination of component parts, everything is constantly changing, and everything is non-substantial. Therefore, everything is empty, all is nothing. Space and time are emptiness, the mirror and the dust are also emptiness. Since the mirror and the dust are both emptiness, how can emptiness collect on emptiness, how can emptiness shine in emptiness?

That is the meaning of the poem and the content of Hui-Neng's realization. The difference between Shen-Hsiu and

Hui-Neng is basically the difference between a dualistic and a non-dualistic outlook. Shen-Hsiu takes his stand on dualism: he distinguishes between the body and the mind, the dust and the mirror, the clean and the unclean. Hui-Neng takes his stand on non-dualism: he sees beyond the duality of subject and object, delusion and enlightenment, dust and mirror. He has seen that both are empty, both are nothing and both are one. In this way he proves himself the true heir of Bodhidharma, who propounded in his own laconic way the same philosophy of nothingness to the Emperor Liang Wu-Ti.

When the Fifth Patriarch Hung-Jen received this stanza from Hui-Neng, he certified the deep realization that had taken place in the mind of his disciple and transmitted to him the patriarchal robe and bowl, the outward sign of the inward transmission of the "Seal of Mind." It is thus that Hui-Neng became the Sixth Patriarch of Zen Buddhism. Why did the Fifth Patriarch choose Hui-Neng as his successor over Shen-Hsiu? Basically, for the same reason that the Buddha chose Mahākāśyapa as his successor over the intellectual Ānanda. There is a difference between intellectual understanding and spiritual realization, and in Zen Buddhism the most important thing is the latter. Both Ānanda and Shen-Hsiu had intellectual knowledge, but they lacked the spiritual insight of a Mahākāśyapa or a Hui-Neng. Shen-Hsiu's dualistic position is perfectly acceptable, even necessary, from the standpoint of intellectual understanding. But Hui-Neng's non-dualistic position is deeper; it goes right to the very bedrock of reality, to the unity underlying differences, to the universal essence flowing through all the ever-changing particulars.

Since everything is interrelated, since all things depend one upon another, nothing is absolute, nothing is separate, but all are part of the one indivisible whole. In this phenomenal world everything has several sides to it: in good there may be bad, in right there may be wrong; in bad there may be good, in wrong there may be right. And these polar opposites are but the two sides of the same coin. The pairs of opposites all exist as part of one reality, and all manifest that one reality. This is similar to the concept of Yin and Yang in Taoism. The Yin and the Yang, the dark or female and the light or male principles, seem opposed to each other. But both are required to complete the harmony of nature, and from the balance of the two the Tao functions and endures. It is the same way in Zen.

Zen would like to lead man to a deep realization of the oneness of everything, to a realization that goes beyond comparison and distinction and overcomes the illusion of separateness. While the Buddha often spoke about suffering and the end of suffering and often distinguished Nirvāṇa from Saṃsāra, the ultimate reality from the phenomenal flux, his deeper teachings lead to the realization that all is one: that "Saṃsāra is Nirvāṇa" and "Delusion is Enlightenment." Thus in the *Avataṁsaka Sūtra,* the crown of Mahāyāna sutras, the Buddha said: "The Mind, the Buddha and sentient beings are not three different things." Hui-Neng also realized this oneness or nothingness, and his realization made him the Sixth Patriarch of Zen Buddhism.

This concept of oneness may be related to everything. What is the beauty of Zen Buddhism? In Zen Buddhism beauty does not lie in brightly colored decorations or in collections of precious objects. The beauty of Zen is found in simplicity and tranquility, in a sense of the all-embracing harmony of things. It is a beauty which reflects the stillness and emptiness that ever dwells in the midst of constant change. The Zen man finds beauty in simple things: in rocks and water, in mosses, plants, sand, ponds and small wooden bridges. These things are simple, yet at the same time very beautiful. A lake reflecting the moonlight, a mountain clothed with mist, a bird

Rocks, water, small trees and a bridge over a *Koi* pond point, in Zen, to the harmonious existence of man and nature.

singing in the sunshine, a rock hiding under the trees, simple things like these delight the man of Zen. Zen art, likewise, strives towards the ideal of simplicity. A Zen artist may render an entire landscape by just a few suggestive brushstrokes. There are many famous Zen paintings which consist of only a single stroke or Chinese character, such as the paintings of "Mu."

As mentioned earlier, when Zen Buddhism took root in China, the concept of meditation came to be interpreted differently than it had been in India. According to the Indian view, meditation always involves sitting in meditation, either in the full-lotus or half-lotus posture. When one is doing something else, then he is not in meditation. Therefore, Bodhidharma and many of the early patriarchs devoted themselves to meditation most of the time every day. Perhaps also for the same reason most Buddhist monks in the Theravāda tradition devote their time largely to chanting, meditation and related religious practices, rather than to other things. But this concept changed in China, especially from the time of the Fifth Patriarch on. Hui-Neng, when he was a disciple of the Fifth Patriarch, did not have time to sit in meditation at all. He was busy cleaning and cooking to support his five hundred friends. But by maintaining mindfulness while working, he was able to bring his mind into the state of meditation and attain a deeper realization than any of his fellow disciples. Through this realization he became the Sixth Patriarch. From the time of Hui-Neng even to the present, Chinese Ch'an and Japanese Zen masters have always emphasized the fusion of meditation and realization with one's daily activities. Meditation should be practiced not only while sitting but also while engaged in work and activity. Therefore, Zen Buddhists in China and Japan do not only sit in meditation. They practice and apply Zen in everyday life.

In this country the number of people who are interested in Zen Buddhism is continually increasing. Many people interested in Zen go to the bookstore and collect many books on Zen Buddhism. Then they go home and read them. Some who view Zen as a subject for scholarly study go to the library and read Zen texts from morning until night. Others earnestly go to whatever Zen lectures they can with a tape recorder in hand, or return home with a notebook full of ideas and bits of information. This is all good. It is good to read and study in order to understand. But if that is all, these people can never understand Zen Buddhism. And why? Because in Zen mere intellectual understanding is nothing—doing is more important. Only by doing can one experience this for himself. He must put into practice the principles he learns from books and from teachers. If a person wants to get a driver's license, he has to learn to drive. There are some people in the West who, when they hear that a great Zen master is coming to this country, get very excited. They try their best to see him and to study with him. That is good. But a Zen master or even a Buddha is just a "finger pointing to the moon." If we want to see the moon of Enlightenment shining in the sky of emptiness, we must see for ourselves. We must walk on the path the master points out. And this he cannot do for us, this we have to do for ourselves.

The truth, reality, Nirvāṇa, can be found everywhere. It is present not only at the Meditation Center or in a temple or in a Zen master, but is present in every particle of dust, in every nook and corner of the universe. Reality is to be found not only during the period of sitting meditation, but all the time, in work as well as in rest, when standing, walking and lying, as well as when sitting. Therefore, in the history of Zen Buddhism there are many cases of Zen masters who experienced enlightenment by hearing the sound of a small rock falling into the bamboo bush, seeing a shadow move across the calm river or the birds coming and going or the clouds appearing and disappearing in the evening sky. Even work can be a means to self-realization. In China there was a famous Zen master during the T'ang dynasty named Pai-Chang. He was the head master of a large monastery and thus worked very hard every day, in meditation, in teaching and in administering the affairs of the monastery. But he also worked very hard with his disciples at manual labor in the fields. One day one of his disciples realized that the Master was growing old. He was afraid that if the Master worked so hard in his old age something might happen to him. Then who would teach, who would take care of the monastery? So one night, out of love for his master, the student hid his tools. When the Master woke up and found his tools missing, he asked around, but no one would show him where his tools were. From that moment on

The unity of different Buddhist traditions is expressed in this formal portrait of monks and nuns participating in the Great Ordination Service, July 1974. Three Venerable Masters from Sri Lanka, Vietnam and the United Kingdom (center front row) were among the preceptors during this ceremony; in which four Bhikkus and Dharma Teachers and three *śramaṇerikas* were ordained.

the Master refused to eat or drink. His disciples grew very worried about him and asked him why he had stopped eating. He replied: "One day without work, one day without food." Needless to say, the Master soon got his tools back.

This story helps us to understand an important aspect of Zen. Some people think that Zen Buddhism is a withdrawal from daily life. They think Zen makes a sharp distinction between everyday affairs and meditation, and asks us to give up the former in order to practice the latter. But this is not the way of Zen. In Zen, when we sit alone in meditation in some quiet place it does not mean that we are isolated and separate from other people. Though physically alone, we are spiritually one with them. And why? Because true meditation is not an affair of the ego-self, but a seeking to break out of the limits of the ego-self and become one with all. Moreover, Zen meditation does not have to be practiced in solitude. We can meditate and attain realization in our daily work, in contact with people, in trying to understand and help them. Truth or reality is everywhere. If we have the capacity to realize it, it is with us everywhere and all the time. One Vietnamese Zen master named Phu-Van of the Ly dynasty taught his disciple, King Tran-Thai-Thon, thus: "Buddha is not in the mountain. Buddha is in everything. If your mind is calm and pure, you can realize Buddha anywhere."

Of course, everybody recognizes that to discipline ourselves in sitting meditation every day is difficult. We make many excuses to ourselves for not meditating. But it is even more difficult to apply meditation to our daily lives. Every day we are working at home, at school, at the office or at our job. If we keep our minds under control, if we can realize the meaning of what we are doing, if we can *be* what we *do*, that is meditation. Every day we face many problems, some easy, some difficult. The difficult problems can cause a lot of trouble. But if we apply the method of meditation—keep the mind calm and quiet in facing the problems—we will find that it will help us. Of course, it is more difficult to apply meditation in action than at rest, but it is also of more value. To love a person when he loves us is easy. But there is also a much greater kind of love, a true love without distinction and without expectation of anything in return, a universal, compassionate love. This love is the compassion that the Buddha taught we should extend to both those who are our friends and those who are not. As we develop in meditation we find we develop more of this universal love. In the same way, when we meet troubles or obstacles in our life, they should be faced with the mind poised in the calm of meditation. We must try to keep the mind straight, calm and clear, we must be courageous; then the problems will

The three bishops who served as the Precept Masters were: Ven. Thich Thien-An, Chief Precept Master from Vietnam (right), Ven. Hsuan-Hua from China, Abbot of Gold Mountain Zen Monastery in San Francisco (left) and Ven. Tsuji from Japan, President of the Buddhist Churches of America (left, second row). In addition to the three Precept Masters and seven Witness Masters, fifteen masters, monks and nuns were present as observers during the Great Ordination Ceremony to support the granting of the precepts.

vanish just as surely as they appear. The sun and moon are always shining. If we can realize the truth, then everywhere is Nirvāṇa.

METHOD OF PRACTICE

As the student becomes adept at mindfulness of breathing meditation, another variation of the practice may be helpful. The first chapter introduced the technique of breath counting. The second chapter described mental visualization of the breaths as they were counted. This practice can be extended one step further: counting, seeing and hearing the breaths. Just as the breaths are visualized with the eyes closed, so the meditator tries to hear the breathing without making any sound. He assumes the regular sitting posture, then breathes lightly and naturally. He keeps his mind on nothing but counting breaths. He does not see anything but breaths, he does not hear anything but breaths. Concentrating on breathing, being aware of breathing, feeling and living breathing, nothing else interferes with the breathing. In other words, one should just be what he is doing. That is the method.

4

Three Essentials of Zen Practice

The past three chapters have been concerned with the history of Zen Buddhism, the teachings of the Buddha, Bodhidharma and Hui-Neng and the spread and development of Zen from India to China, Japan and other Asian countries. From this historical approach we turn to a more topical one, dealing with those aspects of Zen which bear upon the conduct of our daily life. For it is here above all that the true meaning and value of Zen Buddhism is to be found.

The interest in Zen Buddhism is increasing rapidly in the United States and other Western countries, especially among the young people. But while many are drawn to Zen at the beginning, not many follow through to the end. Why is this? Because their interest was not built upon a secure foundation. Lacking a secure foundation, many give up their pursuit of Zen halfway. Their interest becomes merely inquisitive; it comes and it goes; easy in, easy out, like changing clothes. In order to

persist in the path of Zen it is necessary at the outset to know
and to cultivate the three essentials of Zen practice.

The first step is great faith (Jap.: *dai-shin-kon*). When we
undertake the practice of Zen, we have to arouse great faith in
the capacity of our mind at the very beginning, and we have to
maintain this great faith throughout our entire practice of Zen.
But the kind of faith called for in Zen Buddhism differs very
much from the kind of faith required in other religions. Other
religions demand that we place faith in a supreme being and
that we give our assent to various propositions concerning his
nature, attributes and deeds; we can call this kind of faith
"faith in the other." In contrast, faith in Zen Buddhism means
faith in ourselves. According to the teaching of the Buddha,
every living being has a Buddha nature, the potential to become a Buddha. We are not yet Buddhas because we have not
discovered that Buddha nature. The great faith spoken about
in Zen Buddhism means faith that the Buddha nature is
present within us and that by cultivating the way taught by the
Buddha we can come to a realization of that Buddha nature.
To realize our Buddha nature is not easy. It calls for relentless
work, a long and difficult struggle within ourselves. Because of
its difficulty many people who begin abandon the way; therefore, there are not many Buddhas in the world. This is why
faith is so necessary. The first and most important thing is that
we believe in our own latent capacity, that we believe in the
seed of enlightenment within us and that we do not abandon
this faith no matter how many obstacles, internal or external,
we meet on the way.

Can we believe that we have the potential to become a
Buddha? Why not? The Buddha was just a man like us. He had
red blood and salty tears; his body and mind were not so very
different from our own. Before his enlightenment he had
passions, worries, conflicts and doubts. But through medita-

tion he cultivated himself and discovered his Buddha nature, thereby becoming a Buddha or Enlightened One. We also, with all our problems, with all our weaknesses, with all our barriers, have the potential to become Buddhas. If we develop this faith and follow it through to the end, there is no barrier so big that it cannot be overcome.

Many people say man is created by the environment. In Zen Buddhism we reply that it is man who creates the environment and, therefore, that it is man who creates himself. Whatever we become as individuals depends upon our own minds. Whatever the world becomes depends upon the collective minds of men. Through the direction of our will, the formative faculty of the mind, we can change the world into a better world and ourselves into better men. There is a saying in Zen Buddhism that "Saṃsāra is Nirvāṇa and Nirvāṇa is Saṃsāra." Whether the world is Saṃsāra or Nirvāṇa depends entirely on our state of mind. If our mind is enlightened, then this world is Nirvāṇa; if our mind is unenlightened, then this world is Saṃsāra, full of pain, sorrow and misery. A Zen master once said that water is of one essence, but if it is drunk by a cow it becomes milk, while if it is drunk by a snake it becomes poison. In the same way whether life is blissful or sorrowful depends on our state of mind, not on the world. So we must seek to transform the mind, to bring it into the awakened state, and this requires at the outset great faith, faith in ourselves and in the latent powers of the mind.

The second step in Zen Buddhism is great doubt (*dai-gi-dan*). The method of Zen is very scientific. In science we are told never to believe anything unless its truth has been demonstrated experimentally. Zen takes the same stand. We are not to believe anything blindly; rather we must demonstrate its truth to ourselves. The Buddha taught that every human being has the Buddha nature. If so, where is this Buddha nature? We have to discover it for ourselves and keep on doubting until we discover it. It does no good merely to parrot the words of the Buddha. We must prove them to ourselves by searching into our minds, as well as into the world around us. Doubt is therefore a very important part of Zen practice. A Zen master, a teacher or a guru can teach many things. Some of his teachings we may believe, others we may not believe. What is accepted and rejected depends upon our judgment. We have the right to judge; in fact, it is best to judge for ourselves. We must follow what we think is good, reject what we think is not good. Though the Zen master teaches methods of practice to his students and guides their development, he never considers himself a mediator between man and Buddha or between Saṃsāra and Nirvāṇa. He considers his methods and teachings to be but a finger pointing to the moon. Just as the finger is used to see the moon, so his teachings are to be used as a guide to see the truth. And once we see the moon we no longer need to follow the direction of the finger. Sometimes the Master may be right, sometimes he may be wrong. Therefore, we must not believe and follow his direction blindly, but check it out through our own knowledge and experience. If it is good for ourselves and for others, then we may believe it.

To give an example: If a person is not very familiar with Los Angeles and loses his direction, he may drive into a gas station and ask the attendant how to get to the address he is seeking. Sometimes the attendant gives the right directions, and the man drives to the place without any trouble. But at other times the driver may be told to go to the west when his better judgment tells him he should be going east. Then what is he to do? Is he to believe the attendant and give up all confidence in himself? Should he not, rather, believe his better judgment and find the right directions somewhere else? Thus if we seek the advice of the gasoline man, we should accept that advice with a pinch of doubt. We should recognize the possibility that while he may be right, he may very well be wrong.

So the second step along the way of Zen is to enquire and to doubt everything until it is checked out. This second step is very helpful. Too much skepticism is not good at all. But there is skepticism, and there is skepticism. There is a kind of skepticism which is rooted in a narrow, mental outlook, which refuses to believe anything and takes a cynical delight in maintaining an attitude of negativity. And then there is the healthy kind of skepticism, the skepticism which is a stepping stone on the road to deeper understanding. If we follow the first kind of skepticism, then we will doubt our own inner potentiality, our own capacity to attain Buddhahood, as well as the efficacy of the practices which are designed to lead us to this goal. This kind of skepticism leads only to a dead end. But if we follow the broader kind of skepticism, keeping the mind open and critically examining things to determine whether they are right or wrong, that can be very helpful. For example, when a Zen master tells the psychologist that meditation can help a person with mental illness or a nervous condition, the psychologist will not believe what he is told without question. He will examine this hypothesis and even check it out with instruments. Only after repeated checking and testing will he come to a conclusion. In the same way, in taking up Zen Buddhism the question should be asked: why should I sit in meditation. If I continue to practice this way, what is the result? Continue to ask, to question and to practice. After a while, if we find that meditation helps to control the mind, that it helps us to understand ourselves and others more, that it leads to calm, to tolerance, to happiness and serenity, then we should continue to practice. If it does not help, then why continue? Perhaps something else would be better. Therefore, we must enquire and doubt, for as the Zen texts say: "Great enlightenment comes from great doubt."

The third basic step is great determination (*dai-fun-shi*). After we have resolved our doubts and are ready to embark upon the course of practice, we must raise up a spirit of strong determination. We must make a firm resolution to plow ahead and to continue to practice despite all the obstacles which may be met on the path. We must vow never to give up but to strive on diligently. To develop great determination we must have patience and self-discipline. If we lack these, when we meet some difficulties in our Zen practice, we will question our capacity to attain enlightenment and soon give up. Then we will never reach our goal. We must not be impatient for results but must discipline ourselves to practice without expectation or anticipation. As Confucius says: "Do not wish for quick results, nor look for small advantages. If one seeks quick results, he will not attain the ultimate goal. If he is led astray by small advantages, he will never accomplish great things." It is generally very difficult for Western people to practice without looking for immediate results. When I was in Japan this past summer, a famous Zen master there told me that recently two Western men had been studying Zen meditation under him. One stayed six months, one a year. Both of them expected short-cuts, and both wanted graduations when they left. The Master explained to them: "The way of Zen is not the way of a university. We do not set apart a certain period of time for study and then receive a graduation. The way of Zen is not a matter of months or years but of a lifetime. Perhaps you may consider me a master, but I consider myself a student and still study and practice every day." Western men are almost always in a hurry. When they come to Zen, they practice very hard at the beginning, but when they do not get quick results they

The Master administers the *keisaku* (Awakening Stick), which symbolizes the sudden awakening into enlightenment. During long periods of meditation, the mind may lose its sharpness and clarity; however, an expert slap with the *keisaku* brings the mind back into focus, paring concentration to a fine hone. Even the sound of a slap may help practitioners to awaken to their own true nature.

quit. So we must not expect short-cuts. If we look for short-cuts, we will not endure.

In this country there are many young people who use drugs, and some claim to have undergone a kind of transcendental experience through drugs which they identify with enlightenment. If drugs are taken, the person may have some unusual experiences, but that is not enlightenment. Zen Buddhism does not promise any short-cuts. The short-cuts may bring quick results, but they do not last long nor do they have a permanent effect in a person's life. In Zen we must discipline ourselves every day, practicing and advancing step by step without ever giving up. Through the practice of Zen meditation not only will we get more genuine experience and realization, but they will stay with us longer. They will be absorbed into the make-up of our being and will, over a period of time, produce considerable changes for the better, culminating in self-realization and enlightenment. And most important, we will have made these changes by ourselves.

There is only one kind of graduation in Zen Buddhism, and that is the attainment of Supreme Enlightenment, when we become Buddhas. But, though we have a Buddha nature, it is not easy to become a Buddha. It is difficult not only for us, but it was also difficult for the Buddha. The Buddha himself said: "In the universe there is not a spot of land as small as a mustard seed where I have not sacrificed my life or have not buried my bones." It is difficult to imagine how many lifetimes the Buddha reincarnated in this universe, cultivating his wisdom and virtue to attain Buddhahood. Innumerable times, not

In a meeting of East and West, the Master observes a Western approach to beginning Zen practice, as Dr. David Nowlis uses a biofeedback apparatus to monitor his own alpha wave pattern during meditation.

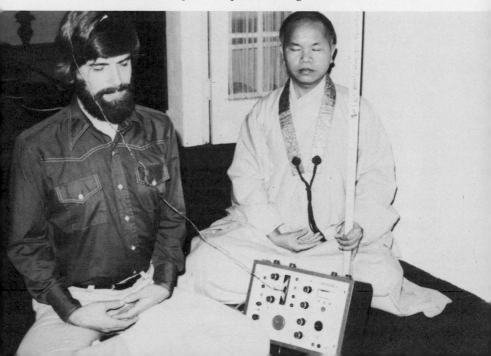

only in the past, but in this life as well, he devoted himself to practice for six years and forty-nine days. Bodhidharma also practiced for nine years after he arrived in China. In this matter, the various Zen masters suggest that, if the mind be thought of as a mirror, "take heed to keep it always clean, and let not dust collect on it." In other words, they suggest that the Zen student diligently practice every day; never cut short, never give up, but continue on.

In the Zen tradition, especially in the monastery life, we usually set apart certain periods for intensive practice of meditation. These periods, called *sesshin* in Japanese, may last for three days, a week, three weeks, three months or longer. During the *sesshin,* the students have set times in which they may interview the master, called *sanzen,* in order to ask questions and to present to the master their understanding and achievements. In most cases, when the student presents his understanding, the master answers: "No, go practice more." He has to say so, for if he says yes, then that is all, there is nothing more. He has to say no to encourage his students to practice. If one does not understand the method of Zen, he will become discouraged and give up, perhaps never to return again. But if he understands this technique, he will not become discouraged but will continue to practice with stronger determination. The answer "no" that the Zen master gives does not necessarily indicate rejection; it is more a way of encouraging the student to move ahead, to try more. The Zen master does not want his disciples to rest satisfied with some minor achievement, but in his compassion wishes to guide them along on the journey from delusion to enlightenment, from Saṃsāra to Nirvāṇa. Therefore, strong determination is most important. Zen meditation is a lifetime process. Just as we breathe and eat every day, so must we meditate every day. Both breathing and eating are important for life, and so is meditation, for meditation keeps our life in balance and helps us understand ourselves and the nature of life. It provides a secure foundation for harmony between ourselves and others, and between ourselves and the universe. So meditation is not a matter of days, weeks, months or years, but of a whole lifetime. And if we have strong determination in our practice, we will, without doubt, reach the final goal, the state of Buddhahood, the realization of perfect wisdom and infinite compassion. As the Zen masters say: "With much clay you can make a large Buddha."

METHOD OF PRACTICE

In Vietnamese Zen a common meditation method is the Recollection of the Buddha, the method of inwardly visualizing an image of the Buddha. The devotee assumes the usual posture and closes his eyes. Then he attempts to visualize the Buddha as clearly as possible. He keeps the image of Buddha before his mind's eye and does not let anything else interrupt it. He tries to see the Buddha as clearly with his eyes closed as he can see physical objects with his eyes open. If he cannot see the Buddha image clearly or if his mind is disturbed by thoughts, he opens his eyes to see the Buddha statue; then once he has a clear mental picture, he closes his eyes and continues again. The Buddha image represents perfect wisdom and compassion. At the beginning of practice the meditator distinguishes the Buddha as the object of meditation from himself as the meditator. But when he has developed this meditation further, both he and the Buddha, subject and object, disappear, and only oneness remains. That oneness is beyond distinction and comparison, beyond the range of sense consciousness. It is quiescent, changeless and perfect. We cannot see it, hear it, touch it or taste it, but it is there; it is always with us; it is perfect wisdom, enlightenment, Nirvāṇa. We can perceive it and live in it only through the calm mind resulting from meditation. Meditation on the Buddha helps to quiet the mind and bring calm to our daily lives.

5

Karma Theory and Zen Buddhism

"How did we get here?" "What made us what we are?" "How can we change ourselves?" "What happens to us when we die?" These are the most fundamental questions we can ask. All thinking men have asked themselves these questions, and the answers they have come up with are as multifarious as men themselves. However, out of the hubbub of speculations on these issues a few alternative replies have emerged, representative of the basic lines of approach. One which has prevailed in the Christian West is the theistic position that a man's destiny is basically determined for him by God. God determines if a man deserves heaven or hell; he may even decide each man's earthly destiny. A second group believes in fatalism. According to fatalism each of us has a fate which we cannot change and about which we can do nothing. As they say, "Whatever will be will be." In this philosophy the agent that determines destiny is not, as in the theistic position, a personal

God, but rather a mysterious impersonal power called "Fate" which transcends our understanding and hence our ability to persuade or manipulate. Again, there is a third group that holds the exact opposite: that everything happens by accident. This is the philosophy of indeterminism. The indeterminist believes that if he is lucky, he will achieve happiness or success; if he is unlucky, he will suffer or fail. But whatever he receives he receives not through any process of determination but by accident, by sheer coincidence.

These three beliefs—theistic determinism, fatalism and indeterminism—are all rejected by Zen Buddhism. So, what answer does Zen offer to the riddle of human destiny? Zen answers with the general Buddhist principle of action and reaction as seen in the sphere of human conduct and experience. According to this law, if a person does something, what he does will inevitably have an effect on him, at present or in the future, and what this effect will be is determined by the character of his original action. If he performs good actions, or good karma, he will reap good results, i.e., happiness and success; if he performs bad actions, or bad karma, he will reap bad results, i.e., suffering and failure. Many are familiar with the words of the Bible: "Ye shall reap what ye shall sow." This quote is precisely the meaning of the law of karma. Except, where Christianity gives this statement a theistic interpretation, Buddhism regards karma as a natural law immanent in the universe. The doctrine of karma is the "middle way" between complete determinism and complete indeterminism.

Buddhism differs significantly from Christianity in another respect. Christianity, while asserting the law of cause and effect, is all too ready to abrogate it by looking for forgiveness through the grace of God and the mediation of a priest. Hence the Christian worships God and prays to Him in order to obtain forgiveness from the results his evil actions hold out for him. But in Buddhism no one can forgive a person for his transgressions. If he commits an evil deed, he has to reap the consequences, for all is governed by universal law and not by any arbitrary creator.

The Buddhist conception of time regards the present, the here and now, as the causal determinant between the past and the future. What we are in the present is the result of what we did in the past, and what we do now in the present determines what we are to become in the future. A Buddhist saying runs thus: "The present is a shadow of the past, the future a shadow of the present." Hence our action in the present is most important, for what we do in the present determines the course of our future development. We should apply our minds to the present so that we may advance on the way. According to the Buddhist doctrine of rebirth, the causal relation between action and its results holds not only with regard to the present life but also with regard to past and future lives. This universal law of cause and effect is ineluctable. Just as we cannot run away from our own shadows, so we cannot run away from the results of our actions. They will pursue us no matter where we hide.

The doctrine of karma is, precisely speaking, not merely a doctrine of cause and effect, but of action and reaction. The doctrine holds that every action willfully performed by an agent—be it of thought, word or deed—tends to react upon that agent. The law of karma is a natural law, and its operation cannot be suspended by any power of a deity. If is as if we violated a traffic law and appealed to the policeman for forgiveness. He would not forgive us, for we have violated the law and must pay the consequences. In the same way, through the working of the law of karma our actions bring about their natural results. Recognizing this, Buddhists do not pray to a god for mercy but rather regulate their actions to bring them into harmony with the universal law. If they do evil, they try to discover their mistakes and rectify their ways; and if they do good, they try to maintain and develop that good.

We should not worry about the past, but rather be concerned about what we are doing in the present. Instead of running around seeking forgiveness, we should try to sow good seeds in the present and leave the results to the law of karma. When a disciple came to the Buddha penitent over past misdeeds, the Buddha did not promise any forgiveness, for he knew that each must reap the results of the seeds that he had sown. Instead he explained: "If you know that what you have done is wrong and harmful, from now on do not do it again. If you know that what you have done is right and profitable, continue to do it. Destroy bad karma and cultivate good karma." We should realize that what we are in the present is a shadow of what we were in the past, and what we will be in the future is a shadow of what we are now in the present. We should apply our minds to the present so that we may advance on the way.

The theory of karma in Buddhism makes man and no one else the architect of his own destiny. From moment to moment we are producing and creating our destiny through our thought, our speech and our deeds. The following verse sums up the essence of the Buddhist position:

> Sow a thought and reap an act;
> Sow an act and reap a habit;
> Sow a habit and reap a character;
> Sow a character and reap a destiny.

Our destiny issues from our character, our character from our habits, our habits from our acts and our acts from our thoughts. And since thoughts issue from the mind, this makes the mind the ultimate determinant of our destiny. In fact, the mind is the only creator Buddhism recognizes, and the power of

During a memorial service held at the International Buddhist Meditation Center following the death of Alan Watts, a young girl expresses her thanks for Dr. Watts' contribution to Zen in the United States.

the mind the only significant power in the world. As Milton says, "The mind can make a heaven of hell, and a hell of heaven." If we think good thoughts, our acts cannot be bad. By thinking good thoughts, we will produce better actions, develop better habits, mold better characters and inherit better destinies. We must not be deceived by the apparently feeble energy of our individual thoughts. Working together slowly and silently, they are the secret agents of all that we are and of all that we might become.

Once a woman in my U.C.L.A. class came to me and said: "I would like to come to your meditation center to practice, but I am too nervous to meditate." I asked her: "Who produces your nervousness? It is yourself. Because you let externals disturb your mind, you become nervous. But if your mind is calm and under control, then nothing can make you nervous, nothing can bother you. Come and practice; then you will find out." She came and learned to control and discipline her mind. As she practiced she gained more confidence in herself, so that events in the outer world no longer disturbed her. Now she is not nervous any more, for she is master of herself and master of her circumstances. Her mind is calm, her mind is quiet. And with a calm, quiet mind, her life is also calm, is also quiet.

Since Buddhism places ultimate responsibility for our life in our own hands, if we want our hands to mold our life in a better way, we must launch our minds in a better direction, for it is the mind which controls the hands which mold our life. But here a question arises. Sometimes we know somebody who is virtuous, gentle, kind, loving and wise, and yet his life is filled with troubles from morning to night. His car breaks down, his children fail in school, he is often sick and out of work. Why is this? What happens to our theory that good acts lead to happiness and bad acts to suffering? To understand this, we must realize that the fruits of karma do not necessarily mature in the same lifetime in which the karma is originally accumulated. Karma may bring about its consequences in the next life or in succeeding lives. If a person was good in a previous life, he may enjoy happiness and prosperity in this life even though his conduct now is bad. And a person who is very virtuous now may still meet a lot of trouble because of bad karma from a past life. It is like planting different kinds of seeds; some will come to flower very fast, others will take a long time, maybe years. The law of cause and effect does not change, but the effects come about at different times, in different forms and at different locations. While some of our experiences are due to karma in the present life, others may be due to karma from previous lives. In the present life, we receive the results of our actions done in past lives as well as in the present. And what we reap in the future will be the result of what we do in the present.

The law of karma binds together the past, present and

future lives of an individual through the course of his transmigration. To understand how such a connection is possible between the experiences and actions of an individual in successive lives, we must take a brief look at the Buddhist analysis of consciousness. According to the Buddhist philosophy of consciousness, the Vijñānavada school, there are eight kinds of consciousness. There are the five sorts of sense-consciousness: i.e., eye, ear, nose, tongue and body consciousness. These make possible the awareness of the five kinds of external sense data through the five sense-organs. The sixth consciousness is the intellectual consciousness, the faculty of judgment which discerns, compares and distinguishes the sense-data and ideas. The seventh consciousness, called the *manas*, is the ego-consciousness, the inward awareness of oneself as an ego and the clinging to a discrimination between oneself and others. Even when the first six kinds of consciousness are not functioning, for example, in deep sleep, the seventh consciousness is still present, and if threatened, this consciousness, through the impulse of self-protection, will cause us to awaken. The eighth consciousness is called the *ālaya-vijñāna*, the storehouse-consciousness. Because this consciousness is so deep, it is very difficult to understand, but its literal name gives us the cue to its meaning. The *ālaya* is a repository which stores all the impressions of our deeds and experiences. Everything we see, hear, smell, taste, touch and do deposits, so to speak, a seed in the store-consciousness. The seed is a nucleus of karmic energy. Since the *ālaya* hoards all the seeds of our past actions, it is the architect of our destiny. Our life and character reflect the seeds in our store-consciousness. If we deposit bad seeds, i.e., perform more evil actions, we will become bad persons. It is as though we were to burn incense in a large hall; then the hall would take on a sweet smell. If we were to bring in some rotten eggs, the hall would take on a foul smell.

The *ālaya*-consciousness not only stores all the seeds, both good and bad, but also carries them from one moment to the next and from the past life to the present life, from the present life to the future life. This is what makes possible the transmission of character, as well as the development or decline of character, over a series of lives. The store-consciousness also explains how, in certain exceptional cases, memories occur of experiences in past lives, or talents and character traits acquired in past lives reach early fruition in the present life. We read of poets, painters and musicians who were creating works of art at a very tender age. We also sometimes hear of children who can speak foreign languages they were never taught by their parents. All these wonders are manifestations of the seed tendencies in the *ālaya-vijñāna*. Our destiny in life is a result of the working out of the karmic seeds in our store-consciousness. This destiny is not predetermined, as fatalism holds, but is rather a product of our own will, through our volitional actions, or karma. If we do good actions, we deposit good seeds in the *ālaya* and will reap good results, and if we do bad actions, we deposit bad seeds and will reap bad results.

Therefore, if we cultivate the way of virtuous conduct, then in the future we will have a better life. As the Buddha teaches in the *Avataṁsaka Sūtra*: "A bodhisattva is concerned about what he does (cause), but not about what he receives (effect). A common man worries about what he receives, but not about what he does." That difference in attitude marks the difference between a Bodhisattva and a common man, and also between a Buddhist and non-Buddhist, a Zen man and a non-Zen man.

Whether something objective is troublesome or not often depends on the state of mind rather than the object itself. If we think that it is trouble, then it is trouble. If we do not think that it is trouble, then it is not trouble. Everything depends on

the mind. For example, sometimes during meditation we are
interrupted by outside noises. If we dwell on them and cling to
them, they will disturb our meditation. But if we dismiss them
from our minds as soon as they arise, then they will not cause a
disturbance. If we are always demanding something out of life,
then we will never be content. But if we accept life as it is,
then we will know contentment. Some people seek happiness
through material things; other people can be happy without
many material things. Why? Because happiness is a state of
mind, not a quantitative measure of possessions. If we are
satisfied with what we are and have now, then we are happy.
But if we are not satisfied with what we are and have now, that
is where unhappiness dwells. The Buddha said that desire is
"bottomless," because no matter how much is put into it, it
can never be filled up—it always remains empty. Thus the *Sūtra
in Forty-two Chapters* says: "Though a person filled with desire
dwells in heaven, still that is not enough for him; though a
person who has ended desire dwells on the ground, still he is
happy."

To establish a better world—a world of peace, harmony and
mutual love between men—we must begin by cultivating our
karma. For the collective karma of the world is nothing but a
reflection of the individual karma of the individuals that make
up the world. To cultivate our karma we must begin with the
mind. For all kinds of action are nothing but outward expressions of what transpires in the mind. If our minds are filled
with hatred, what will happen? We will make many enemies.
But if our minds are filled with love, what will happen? We
will make many friends. What stirs in the heart reveals itself
outwardly in the world. Thus everything depends upon the
heart of man. Confucius expresses the same idea when he says:

> If there be righteousness in the heart, there will be beauty
>   in the character,

If there be beauty in the character, there will be harmony
    in the home,
If there be harmony in the home, there will be order
    in the nation.
If there be order in the nation, there will be peace
    in the world.

If we wish to have a peaceful world, we must begin by improving ourselves; we must cultivate our persons and rectify
our hearts. If we improve ourselves, then we can build up a
happy and harmonious family life. When a nation is made up
of harmonious families, then the nation will be well-ordered.
And with well-ordered nations we can establish peace in the
world.

In the West it is sometimes believed that if we want peace
we must secure it by force; as politicians frequently say, "We
must *win* the peace." In the Orient, especially in Buddhism, we
believe that the way to peace lies through peace: we must
develop peace within ourselves if we hope to establish peace in
the world. We can never attain peace by fighting with each
other, by killing each other. The road to peace begins in the
heart. The condition of the world is the product of the deeds,
words and thoughts of the people that make up the world. If
everyone practices better action, better speech and better
thought, then the world will be exactly that much better. In
order to achieve peace we must learn, above all, to be more
tolerant. We must learn to respect the differences between
people, to see that points of view alien to our own may be valid
to those who hold them. Too often we are inclined to believe
that a peaceful society must be a homogeneous society, a
society where everyone thinks, acts and speaks alike. However,
it is better to have a variegated society, provided we can come
to recognize that variety does not of necessity exclude harmony. In music, in order to achieve harmony there must be

different notes; if all notes are the same, what results is not harmony but monotony. Variety is more than the spice of life: it is the very substance of meaningful existence.

The theory of karma in Buddhism thus teaches that man is the creator of his own life and his own destiny. All the good and bad that comes our way in life is the result of our own actions reacting upon us. Our joys and sorrows are the effects of which our actions, both in the distant and the immediate past, are the causes. And what we do in the present will determine what we become in the future. Since man is the creator of his own life, to enjoy a happy and peaceful life he must be a good creator, that is, he must create good karma. Good karma comes ultimately from a good mind, from a pure and calm mind. When we sit in meditation, we produce a pure and calm mind; this is the cause. And from this pure and calm mind comes a calm life, a peaceful life, a happy life; this is the effect. Meditation is not simply a form of mental relaxation. It is something more. It is a way of transcending our finite ego-selves, of realizing our True Self which is Non-Self, of finding the ultimate reality that lies within, of creating better thought as the indispensable foundation for building a better life and a peaceful world.

METHOD OF PRACTICE

A very effective meditation practice which helps to create good thought and karma is the meditation of loving-kindness. Love in Buddhism differs from the devotional love of the theistic religions, which is directed to a supreme being or god believed to stand above man and to control his destiny. And Buddhist love also differs from the common type of love, or worldly love, which is an exchange love that works on the principle "if you love me, I will love you." Loving-kindness in

Buddhism is an impartial and universal love, free from every trace of egocentric grasping. It extends to all beings, making no distinction between friend and enemy, between man and animal, nor even between oneself and others. In order to develop this kind of love, meditation is necessary. The meditator who cultivates this practice sits in the usual meditation posture, breathing in and out lightly and naturally, keeping his mind calm. Then he radiates loving-kindness outward to others. He tries to feel genuine love for them and share the warmth of this love with them. He feels them as his own; he breathes and lives with them. It is best to begin the meditation by radiating this loving-kindness to everybody in the room, then to all mankind, then to everything and every being in the universe. Then the meditator develops this love on a deeper level, where he makes no distinction between himself and others. Here there is no subject and no object, no one to love and no one to be loved, but only love, boundless and without measure. That is the kind of love which develops from a state of deep meditation and which expresses itself in the Bodhisattva vow to save all sentient beings however innumerable they may be. Meditation on loving-kindness produces better karma of thought, speech and deed, developing a better person and contributing towards the great work of universal compassion.

6

The Way of Action

As the last chapter explained, thought plays an important role in Zen Buddhism. According to Zen, the formation of our destiny lies ultimately in our own minds, in the process of thought which in its accumulative power builds up for us our habits, our character and our destiny. But thought alone is not enough to put a formative stamp upon our personality. For thought to be of value, Zen holds, it must be translated into action: understanding, while important, is nowhere near as important as acting. Therefore, to understand Zen, one must see the role of action in Zen Buddhism. For Zen Buddhism is not so much a theoretical philosophy to be discussed and debated at leisure as it is a way of action, a philosophy to be practiced and realized every moment of our daily life.

To attain the experience of enlightenment, which is the goal of Zen Buddhism, sitting in meditation is necessary, but the practice of meditation is by no means the completion or the total substance of the Zen Buddhist life. Meditation serves to develop wisdom, but we must be able to give concrete expression to this wisdom, and to do so we have to cultivate right action. Many people think that the Zen Buddhist turns his back upon the world to submerge himself in abstract meditation. This is a misconception. If everybody were to sit in meditation all the time, who would take care of us, of our family, our community, of the world? To practice Zen is to make the practice of sitting meditation an integral part of our daily life, but it is at the same time to work, to act with loving-kindness and respect for others, to contribute our part to the world in which we live in order to change this world into a better world. The Zen way is not to withdraw from life into an isolated utopia, but to get into life and change it from the inside by action.

The following story illustrates the importance of action in Zen Buddhism. Once in ancient China, there lived a great Buddhist scholar. He had studied the scriptures with diligence, knew whole passages by heart and could expound the texts at length both by mouth and by pen. Yet, despite his learning, he had fallen into confusion because of the many contradictory things he encountered in his studies. He went from one teacher to another seeking to resolve his doubts, but this only left him more confused. Then one day he heard that a famous Zen master was residing in a nearby temple. He went to see the Master and, after greeting him respectfully, asked: "Could you please tell me, Venerable Sir, what is the essence of Buddhism? I have read many books and have only become confused. Please help to resolve my doubts." The Master smiled at him and replied: "I too have read many books and practiced for many years, but cannot tell you anything of my own. But let me recite for you a little *gāthā* ("poem") which may contain the answer you are seeking." The scholar was delighted, and the master recited:

> Not to commit evils,
> To practice all the good,
> And to keep the mind pure:
> That is the teaching of the Buddhas.

The scholar immediately exclaimed: "What, is that all you have to answer? Why, any child of three knows that!" "True," the Master answered, "any child of three knows that, but even an old man of eighty finds it difficult to practice." This statement suddenly made sense to the scholar. He realized that studying treatises on philosophy is not the key to understanding Buddhism; the key lies rather in practice. Joyfully he expressed his gratitude to the Master and returned home, his mind at last set at rest.

To perform one's daily activities in the Zen spirit, one should perform them as forms of meditation. We should not meditate only when we sit in quiet but should apply the method of meditation to our daily life. When we wash dishes, we must meditate. When we work in the garden, meditate. When we drive, meditate. When we do business, meditate. In other words, we must meditate at every moment, in every activity of our daily life. Hui-Neng, while working in the kitchen to support his five hundred friends in the monastery, attained a deep realization and was finally chosen by the Fifth Patriarch Hung-Jen as his successor. When taking care of our daily affairs, we should distinguish the good from the evil and practice the former and abstain from the latter. But what is good and what is evil? Good and evil are defined differently in different religions, but Zen offers a very simple explanation. In Zen Buddhism an action is considered good when it brings happiness and well-being to oneself and others, evil when it brings suffering and harm to oneself and others. We must not create suffering for others. And why? Because, according to Zen, we ourselves and others are not different, but are related to each other by bonds more intimate than we can suspect. We are in reality extensions of each other. You are my extension, and I am your extension. Therefore, Zen suggests that we take others into consideration before we act and speak, regarding them as we regard ourselves.

Many religions urge people to do good to others, to be loving, kind and charitable. But Zen introduces a very unique concept into its notion of virtue. This is the concept of the "deed of no merit." An illustration may explain what this "deed of no merit" is. If a person goes to church, the priest or minister may announce to the congregation that he has some plans for the future and ask for contributions to realize these plans. In front of the priest and congregation, one man may raise his hand and say: "I contribute $1000." This may come very easily to him. But it is quite a different matter when the same person is asked to give $10 to a needy person when nobody else is watching. Many people like to do good, providing that they can at the same time receive credit for doing good. Even Jesus, though he urges his disciples not to let their left hand know what their right hand is doing, comforts them by saying, "Thy Father who seeth in secret shall reward thee." This is not yet a deed of no merit. As long as the thought of any reward, whether open or secret, is present, the deed is, from the viewpoint of Zen, not yet thoroughly pure, but is still marked by tracks and shadows. For a deed to be totally pure, it must be done without any thought of reward, whether worldly or divine. It is this kind of deed which is called a "deed of no merit." And because no merit is sought, it is a deed of immeasurable merit, of infinite merit.

For a deed to be great, it is not necessary that it be

grandiose. What is important is the motive behind the deed
and not the magnitude of the deed itself. If the motive is pure,
then the deed is pure; if the motive is impure, then, no matter
how large the deed is, it is still impure. Perhaps this is why,
when Emperor Wu-Ti asked Bodhidharma how much merit
he had acquired for promoting Buddhism in a large-scale way,
Bodhidharma replied: "No merit at all." On the other hand, a
small deed that proceeds from a pure heart may amass an
incalculable store of merit. On the day that Śākyamuni Buddha
was to enter Parinirvāṇa, all his disciples journeyed to the town
where the Buddha lay in rest in the hope of seeing him for the
last time. Monks, nuns and laymen gathered from all directions, many of them having made long pilgrimages over the
difficult Indian terrain. Because it was their last chance to see
the Buddha, the disciples brought with them the best gifts
they had to offer to the Buddha: food, clothes, flowers, fruit,
incense, candles, etc. They burnt incense and lit candles, praying for the Buddha to remain alive until all arrived. As the
crowds gathered around the Buddha, light connected with
light, so that by nightfall the thousands of candles burning together created an ocean of light which dispelled the
thickening darkness. At the moment the Buddha passed away,
suddenly the weather changed. A storm struck up with a
strong wind that swept across the crowd. The wind blew out
all the lights except one small candle far behind in the corner.
This small candle remained lit no matter how heavily the wind
blew. All the people gazed at it with astonishment and wonder.
When the storm was over, it was discovered that the candle
belonged to an old lady. This lady was very poor. She did not
have anything to eat or drink all the way from her house to the
place where the Buddha lay at rest. She had only one small coin
in her pocket, and though she was hungry and thirsty, she used
her coin to buy a small candle to offer to the Buddha. This was

the candle which remained burning through the wind and rain of the storm.

To do good, we do not have to do spectacular deeds. Just as tiny drops of water can fill a bucket over a period of time, so can small deeds, repeatedly performed, build up a character of highest virtue. Zen suggests that we begin with ourselves by doing small acts of good. For example, when we walk, we should always look down at our feet. There are many living beings that crawl on the ground. If we are careless in walking, we may kill an ant or some other kind of bug. So Buddhism suggests that we look down and be careful when we walk. This is especially difficult to do because there is nobody to check on us and blame or praise us. There are many people who do good when they are in the company of others but not when they are alone. Zen teaches us to do good even when we are alone. When we see a broken bottle on the street, we should remove it so that it cannot hurt anyone. When we are walking alone, we should be careful to take a longer step to save the ant on our path. To give to the poor, to help the needy, to care for the sick, these are little ways of benefitting others which are, in their own way, great. In Vietnamese Buddhism there is a saying: "One mouthful when hungry is better than a full bowl when not hungry." Furthermore, giving does not have to be material. A smile, a kind word, a compassionate thought— these are ways of giving too, and these can be more important and more effective than material gifts. In giving one should not discriminate between great and small, but simply give. The value of giving is based on quality, not quantity. And many small acts of giving can produce great results. As we say, one tree cannot make a wood, but two trees can become a forest. If we are to know more about the *gāthā*, "Not to commit evils and to practice all good," we must start from these small points. To do such is a great achievement.

The third line of the *gāthā* states: "To keep the mind pure." Our minds are always full of thoughts—some very good, some not so very good. If we want to attain self-realization, we must keep our minds pure. According to the *Awakening of Faith*, our store-consciousness, or mind, has two aspects, the pure and the impure. If daily we try to eliminate the impure part and cultivate the pure, then gradually our mind will change until only the good and pure remains; our store-consciousness will be transformed into Tathāgatha consciousness, and we will attain Buddhahood. This shows us the importance of a pure mind: if the mind is pure, then everything becomes pure. The Buddha was originally a man like us, but by eliminating all evil, cultivating all good and purifying his mind he became a Buddha, an Enlightened One. This is the method not only of Śākyamuni Buddha but of all the Buddhas of the past, present and future. The most effective way of keeping the mind pure is by sitting in meditation. We ought to discipline the mind to abide in purity by sitting in meditation every day, morning and night. We must not let laziness become our excuse. Nevertheless, to practice Zen we must not withdraw from life, but get into life: we must fulfill our duties, do what we have to do for others, contribute our part to the whole so as to change this world into a better world. We must not think that we are alone. There are many people in this world quietly trying to fulfill the Way, our unknown companions on the path. Everywhere are Bodhisattvas who will be our friends and guide us through the storm of troubles. The power we each have as a single individual is great, for our influence can radiate outward and bring others within its fold. Thus our family, our community, our nation and our world will gradually become better.

Emperor Aśoka was a great ruler of ancient India, an ardent Buddhist responsible for propagating Buddhism throughout

India and the surrounding regions of the civilized world. Before he became a Buddhist he had conquered many people and had led victorious armies into many lands. But after his conversion to Buddhism, he said: "To conquer others is not difficult. To conquer oneself is more difficult." What did he mean by conquering oneself? He meant the conquest of desire, of attachment, of emotion. If we conquer ourselves, our speech, action and thought always will be good. To conquer ourselves we must sit in meditation. In meditation we do not let desire, attachment or hatred triumph over us, but we battle and triumph over them. And by conquering ourselves, we can best help others conquer themselves.

The way of Zen is the way of action. To benefit ourselves and to benefit others, that is to practice the way of Zen. Abstain from evil and practice good, that is the teaching of all the Buddhas. Every day, in the home, on the street, at work or at school, a thousand occasions present themselves to us for

Leading students in chanting meditation, Rev. Thich Hong-Quang, a Vietnamese *bhikkhu,* plays the bell and *mokkyō* ("wooden fish"). These two musical instruments are found in every Zen temple.

cultivating the path to Buddhahood. We must not let the small size of the deeds blind us to their vast significance. It is by a thousand drops of water that a bucket is filled. If we begin to collect the drops now, we will soon find our bucket brimming over with water.

METHOD OF PRACTICE

An unusual method of meditation was taught by the Buddha in the *Sūrangama Sūtra*, a major text in Mahāyāna Buddhism. In this sutra the Buddha attempted to awaken his disciples to the true nature of hearing by striking a bell and asking them to trace the sound to the mind, which is the source of hearing and sound. The meditator, sitting in meditation posture, strikes the bell. He then tries to hear it as long as he can. He then thinks: Who is hearing? What is the nature of the sound? He uses his ears to hear the sound of the bell and his mind to find out the true nature of the sound and the true mind to realize the true Self. After the bell is struck, the sound gradually dissipates and eventually disappears; then, through meditation, the meditator tries to trace where the sound goes. If sometimes the sound of silence, the sound of no sound, can be heard, then why not hear the sound of the bell when it is not hit? Of course, we cannot use our two ears to hear that sound, just as we cannot use our two ears to hear the sound of one hand clapping.

To practice this method at home, the disciple finds a small bell which, when hit gently, gives out a sound that reverberates for a long time. He then listens to the sound of the bell and restrikes it when he can no longer hear it. Where does the sound come from and where does it go? Who is hearing it?

7

Self-Reflection
in Zen Buddhism

Man is distinguished from the beast primarily by his capacity for self-knowledge. Both men and animals eat, sleep and reproduce; both experience sensations, emotions and perceptions; and both are capable of gathering information about the external world. But only man is truly capable of knowing himself. This fact was clearly recognized by the great Western philosopher Socrates, who took as the cornerstone of his philosophy the maxim: "Know thyself." Zen Buddhism concurs in this recognition of self-knowledge as the distinguishing mark of authentic human existence. Unlike the Western theistic religions, Zen is not concerned with knowledge of a God. And unlike modern science, Zen is not concerned with factual knowledge about the external world. What occupies the primary place in the search for knowledge in Zen Buddhism is we ourselves: ever present, and yet so far away; so close at hand, and yet so elusive; so familiar, and yet so poorly understood.

To know ourselves is first of all to know that our own true nature is the Buddha nature. Just as the sun and moon are always shining, but may not be visible because they are obscured by clouds and mist, so the Buddha nature is ever present within us, though it may not be apparent because it is covered over by the clouds of lust, hatred and delusion. To practice meditation is to remove the layers of clouds that conceal our true being so that our Buddha nature may appear again, wonderful and radiant in its intrinsic purity. When the Buddha attained Supreme Enlightenment under the Bodhi tree, he laughed. Why? Because before he was enlightened he thought the truth he was seeking was something distant from himself. But when he achieved Enlightenment, he realized that the truth he sought was nothing other than his true nature, which was ever with him before the beginning of time. The whole process of Saṃsāra, of wandering through the painful round of birth and death, had begun merely because he had lost sight of his original nature. But his true nature had never departed from him, and when he became enlightened, he discovered that is was ever present, only needing his recognition to become apparent.

To illustrate this truth, the Buddha related the following story in the *Lotus Sūtra*: Once in India there lived a family which consisted of a man, his wife and their son. The parents were very rich; they owned many acres of land and had a large sum of money in the bank and great quantities of gold and jewels. However, their son was not very intelligent. The parents often worried about what would happen to him after they died, for he was so simple-minded that they did not think him capable of managing his own affairs. Then one day the father had an idea. He gave his son a precious jewel of inestimable value and told him to keep the jewel tied up in his clothes. He was never to take it out until they died. Only then could he remove it, sell it in the marketplace and use the money he received to support himself. The son bore his father's words in mind and kept the promise. Then one day, as the years passed by, his father died; several years later his mother died, and the son came by his full inheritance. In his ignorance, however, the young man foolishly squandered his wealth on fruitless pursuits. He sold the furniture, the houses, the rice fields, the granaries and all else, but while he spent, he did not earn. Thus, before he knew it, he found himself a poor man, without a penny to his name, without even a roof over his head. He was reduced to the state of a beggar, wandering from house to house and from town to town begging for his meals. Some days he got enough to eat, but on other days he got no food at all. One day, overcome by hunger and exhaustion, he lay down in the middle of the street, too weak and tired to move. Just then a Buddhist monk walked down the street and saw the young man lying on the ground. The monk began to help the man to his feet when suddenly a wonderful precious jewel fell out of the shredded clothing. "Why are you begging for food," the monk asked, "when all the time you have had this precious jewel? Go sell it, and use the money to support yourself." The young man was struck with wonder and amazement at seeing this jewel he had forgotten about for so long. He sold it in the market, and with the money he got for it he was able to buy back all his former possessions. Never again did he have to suffer from poverty.

The young man in the story always carried the jewel with him. It was only because he had forgotten about it that he had to suffer from poverty, hunger and disease. When he discovered that the jewel was always with him, he was able to wipe out all his troubles. In the same way, we always carry about within ourselves the precious jewel of the Buddha nature, but because of our ignorance we do not perceive it and so undergo

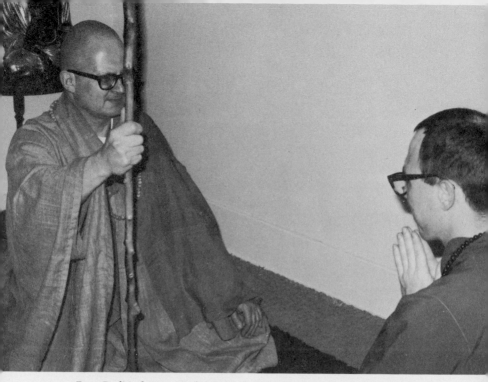

Rev. Bodhi, former head monk of the International Buddhist Meditation Center, Los Angeles, is shown in an interview (*sanzen*) with visiting Zen Master, Ven. Song-Ryong Hearn.

the sufferings of birth and death. But when suddenly we become enlightened, we realize the Buddha nature was with us from the very beginning, and thereby we wipe out all the afflictions that have troubled us since we began the round of birth and death. The Buddha nature is not something distant: it is the bright and precious substance of our original mind.

But though the Buddha nature is present within us, we are not yet Buddhas. The reason we are not yet Buddhas is because we are still victims of the ego-delusion. Our minds are continually dominated by a seemingly endless train of egocentric thoughts—thoughts of greed, attachment, anger, pride, envy and passion. Self-reflection not only awakens us to the immaculate Essence of Mind, abiding silently in the mind's depths, but also brings to our attention the hordes of deluded thoughts that clutter its surface. It is only by becoming cognizant of our weaknesses through self-reflection that we can work to remove the roots from which they spring. It is only by careful analysis of the functionings of our minds that we can discover in ourselves the negative factors which hinder enlightenment and the positive factors which are conducive to enlightenment. Through this self-knowledge, we are prepared to undertake the work of self-cultivation, which involves removing the negative forces and cultivating the positive forces. Self-reflection opens to our eyes the secret contents of our inner life and is thus an indispensable tool in the process of self-transformation which constitutes the heart of Buddhism.

A simple story shows the importance of self-reflection in daily life. In ancient China there were many pious Buddhist families in which the religious life of Buddhism was shared by all the members of the family. But in more recent times a generation gap set in between the parents and their children. The parents might be very devout Buddhists while their children regarded them as old-fashioned and superstitious. In one such family the parents chanted sutras, practiced meditation, recited the name of the Buddha and often went to the temple to hear Dharma-masters speak the Dharma and explain the sutras. The son, however, would have none of these activities. He regarded Buddhism as a mass of superstition, ritual and fantasy, and was himself interested only in science, technology and the materialistic lures of modern life. The son continually pleaded with his parents to give up their Buddhist ideas. He criticized the concepts of Buddhist philosophy and mocked the practices in which his pious parents participated. One day, after his parents returned from temple, his father called his son to his room and spoke to him thus: "Son, it seems you are not happy to see your mother and me go to the Buddhist temple so often. You always criticize our religion. Would you like us to stop going to the temple?" The son nodded his assent. "Well, I'll tell you something," the father continued, "We will never go to the temple again." The son became excited. "Providing that you could do for me one small favor. Are you willing to do it?"

"O yes, Father, I would do anything to get you to throw off that religious nonsense."

"Go to the store now, and buy yourself a pencil and a small notebook. Then from today on, for the next week, I would like you to sit down for one hour a day, let your mind flow and write down in the notebook every idea that comes into your mind—every plan, every desire, every memory. The only thing I ask is that you do this honestly, with complete candor. Then come to me at the end of the week, and show me the notebook. Do you promise to do this?"

The son, thinking this was an easy task, readily agreed. "You also keep your promise," he added. The father nodded.

That night the son sat down at his desk and began to write. He wrote with complete honesty, not holding anything back. One moment this thought came into his mind—he wrote it down; the next moment that thought came into his mind—he wrote it down. He wrote down all his hopes and dreams and fantasies, all his desires and regrets and fears and memories. Thus he continued one hour each night for three nights. Then, on the third night, as he lay on his bed, curiosity began to grow in him. He started to wonder what he had written in the past few days. His curiosity grew stronger and stronger until he could not sleep, but jumped up and began to read. As he read through his notebook, a burning sense of shame overwhelmed him. He felt a pain gnaw at the heart as he poured through the pages he had written. He thought of his mother and his father and of their love for him, and all this provoked in him a disgust for his inward state of being, the state which he had candidly revealed in the pages of his notebook. Too ashamed to show the book to anyone, he threw it into the fire and watched over it until it was all consumed. Then he went to see his father.

He found his father sitting in meditation before the Buddha altar in the shrine room. He entered and sat quietly behind him. After the father completed his meditation, he turned around and saw his son. Sensing that something was wrong, he asked: "What is the matter with you, my son?"

"You've won the game, Father."

"What game?"

"Well," the son explained, "you asked me to write down all my thoughts and feelings one hour a day in a notebook. I kept my promise and did so honestly. Tonight I looked over my notebook and realized that I cannot show it to you. There are some thoughts and feelings I have that are just too private and of which I am too ashamed. Now I am aware that there is a great deal of imperfection in myself. I see that it is necessary to practice Buddhism to purify myself. Next time you go to the temple, please let me go with you."

This story clearly shows us the necessity for practicing meditation and cultivating the Way. Within the privacy of our minds pass many thoughts we would not reveal even to our closest friends and dearest loved ones: our minds are filled with dark tracks and shadows. It is no solution to conceal these thoughts from others and from ourselves, for the impulses they spring from still remain and haunt us in the depths of our inner being. The only solution is to pursue the evil thoughts to their roots in the mind and extricate the roots themselves; then our minds will become pure and clear. The first step in this process is to become aware of our faults. So long as we are blind to our faults, no self-cultivation can take place at all, for our passions, hatreds and delusions are the material upon which self-cultivation works. The father skillfully led his son into taking this step of recognition by asking him ro record with complete candor all his thoughts and feelings. Once the awareness of our flaws impresses itself upon our mind with enough force, there will arise in us the desire to be free from them. This is where the real work of meditation begins, with the purification and perfection of the mind. Our mind is just like a room. If we burn incense in the room, it will become fragrant, but if we allow garbage to fester in it, it will become putrid. In the same way, our mind has two sides to it, the good and the bad, the beautiful and the ugly, the pure and the impure, and we are free to develop it in either of these two directions. To practice Buddhism is to work at eliminating the bad and increasing the good. When we accomplish this, when we become thoroughly pure and good, then we will be Buddhas, Enlightened Ones endowed with wisdom and compassion.

The most difficult part of self-reflection is learning to be critical towards oneself. It is easy to be swept away by pious emotions and enthusiasm for the religion of one's conviction. It is much more difficult to keep an eye on our faults and hindrances and to keep them in check. But this work is absolutely essential, for without exertion there can be no progress on the path—no *samādhi*, no wisdom, no enlightenment, no Nirvāṇa. When we are asked to keep an eye on our own faults, we usually find our eyes focused upon the faults of others. We are more tolerant of ourselves than we are of other people. We are like the woman who continually pointed to the dust on other people's windows while she did not notice that her own window was covered with dust. We should follow Shen-Hsiu's advice and keep the dust from settling on the clear mirror of the self nature. Buddhism teaches that before we criticize other people for keeping dirty apartments we should learn to tidy up our own first. Before we pass judgment on the other man, we should examine ourselves and ask whether we are perfect. As the Buddha says: "Let not one seek others' faults, things left done and undone by others, but one's own deeds done and undone." If we are not yet perfect, why should we expect others to be more perfect than we are. The other man is human also, and so, being human, he is liable to commit mistakes. If we reflect along these lines, it is easy to be tolerant towards other people when we are confronted by their errors, weaknesses and shortcomings. But while we should be tolerant towards others, we should not be too tolerant towards ourselves. When we become too tolerant towards ourselves, we tend to overlook our faults, and when we overlook our faults, we cannot purify ourselves or make any progress on the path. Self-reflection must enable us to discover both our positive and negative qualities so that we can cultivate the former and eliminate the latter. In this way, little by little we advance along the path of moral and spiritual perfection. Each period we sit in meditation we create good thought, a pure and quiet mind; from that our actions, habits and character will be pure, and from that we will enjoy a happier and more meaningful life.

METHOD OF PRACTICE

A most effective method to perceive our mind as it really is, is the meditation Bodhidharma introduced when he brought Zen Buddhism from India to China. This method is called in Chinese *pi-kuan*, "wall-contemplation," and means sitting in meditation facing a wall. Facing the wall signifies that in meditation we are looking inward rather than outward. This is the more introspective type of meditation practiced today by the Soto school of Zen in Japan.

The disciple sits in the meditation posture with his face turned toward the wall. He does not think of anything and so does not create any thoughts. If thoughts arise, he does not worry, does not pay attention to them, but just relaxes his grip on them and they disappear of themselves. Whatever arises passes away. He continues to meditate with a calm and quiet mind, making no distinction between subject and object. This is the method of "no-thought," *mu-nen* in Japanese. Dogen Zenji, founder of Soto Zen in Japan, said: "Sitting in meditation (*zazen*) and enlightenment (*satori*) are one." So if we sit in meditation with our mind free from thoughts, we will quickly reach enlightenment.

8

Mu

One cannot study Zen without looking at the concept of Mu. The term Mu, which means "emptiness" or "nothingness," has become best known as a *koan* in Rinzai Zen, "Joshu's Mu," and it can indeed be said that the whole aim of all schools of Zen is to bring about the realization of Mu. However, the origin of this concept (which spells the end of all concepts) goes back to the very basic teaching of the Buddha. The Buddha taught that all phenomena are branded with four salient marks: impermanence (*anitya*), suffering (*duḥkha*), selflessness (*anātma*) and emptiness (*śūnyatā*).

The first mark of impermanence is evident from the ever present fact of change. No entity, according to Buddhism, ever remains static even for a single moment; its very being is a process of becoming, and just as surely as this process had a beginning, it will have an end. The second mark of suffering reveals that no conditioned thing is fully satisfactory, but that

either overtly or dormantly all conditioned things are sources
of suffering. The fact of suffering is apparent in birth, old age,
illness and death, in separation from the pleasant, contact with
the unpleasant and in the frustration of our desires. In brief,
the whole body-mind complex composed of the five *skandhas* is
suffering. The third mark of selflessness points out that there is
no permanent self, soul or ego behind the ever changing flux of
mental and physical processes that comprise our being. A
living being is a compound of the five *skandhas* of form,
sensation, perception, volitional formations and consciousness,
and neither behind nor within these five aggregates can any
ego-entity be found. The fourth mark is Mu: emptiness. All
phenomena, the Buddha says, are Mu, empty and void. Why
does the Buddha say this? Because all phenomena arise and
exist through the combination of many different elements.
Since whatever exists depends upon other things for its existence, it lacks an immutable core of independent actuality and
is therefore, considered in itself, void. Phenomena possess a
kind of apparent existence, in that they can be seen, heard,
touched, etc., but beyond their status as appearances they have
no substantial reality. This lack of substantial reality is what is
signified by the word Mu.

Perhaps this difficult concept of emptiness can be clarified
by one or two illustrations. If in a dark room a stick of burning incense is twirled very rapidly, a circle of light is seen. But
as soon as the incense stops moving, the circle disappears.
Though the circle was visible and everybody saw it as such, it
was actually an illusion created by the mind. Since it has no real
existence, the circle even when present and visible is empty: it
is Mu. In the same way, all phenomena are empty because they
arise in dependence upon causes and conditions. In themselves
they are as vacuous and insubstantial as the circle created by the
twirling stick. Again, phenomena are empty because they are

evanescent. Things perish the moment they arise, and thus there is no abiding entity behind the sensible appearances that present themselves to us. The phenomenal universe is like a film projected upon a blank screen. The film is a continuous series of ever changing pictures. Through our ignorance we may become attached to the figures on the screen. We may laugh with them or cry with them, swell with pride or grow tense with excitement, but this does not make them real, and once the projector stops, all these figures with whom we have been so deeply involved will vanish into nothingness, together with all their loves and hates, their joys and sorrows, their adventures and intrigues. The world is just like a movie on the screen: evanescent, insubstantial and void. Even this very being we call our "self" dissolves upon analysis into a mere appearance destitute of final actuality.

Our being is a combination of different elements. The body is a compound of the four primary elements—solidity, fluidity, vibration and heat—and the mind is a compound of sensations, conceptions, volitions and consciousness. Further, the body and mind are constantly changing. The weak, hesitant boy turns into the vigorous young man, the vigorous young man into the doting elder, and no factor in this process is permanent and unchanging. Hence there is no self to be grasped as an ego.

From here we can take a step deeper into the understanding of Mu. At the first step we see that everything is empty. This is the stage where, in the words of the *Heart Sūtra*, there dawns upon us the realization that "form is emptiness." When we understand this, we will see into the realm of non-differentiation where distinctions vanish and all things merge into one undifferentiated essence, the Void. But this step, if posited alone, would lead into the philosophy of nihilism. Since differences are denied, the implication seems to be that moral values may be turned topsy-turvy without any dire consequences; the result would be moral and intellectual chaos. Therefore, in the second step Zen asserts that although all things are empty, still at its own level the realm of differentiation, together with the laws which determine its structure, possesses a kind of validity. This step is described by the *Heart Sūtra* as the realization that "emptiness is form." At this level once again you are you, and I am me. You have your property and I have mine, and I cannot very well take yours without your permission just as you cannot take mine without my permission. Thus the second step brings us back to the world of empirical reality where each man is responsible for his own conduct and where each man will be held responsible for his conduct through the inevitable working of the law of karma.

The first and final goal of Zen Buddhism is to realize that everything is Mu. But this realization must be experiential, not merely intellectual. It is not enough to assert that everything is empty; one must see into the fact of emptiness in all one's daily activities. Emptiness is to be grasped from the inside at each moment it presents itself, which is every moment, without a moment's hesitation. As soon as one hesitates, gives rise to a doubt or a deluded thought, emptiness has packed its bags and gone a million miles away; then one's self-ascribed enlightenment may be valued as naught.

Once there was Zen student who was studying the *koan* "Mu" under a master. He worked very hard on the *koan* for several years until, one evening in meditation, he believed that he had realized *satori*. He ran to the Master to report his experience, but the Master was not in a hurry to offer his

Opposite: "Calligraphy of Mu," emptiness, the most important insight in Zen, was executed by the Rinzai Zen Master, Abbot of Shōung-In Temple in Tokyo, and given to the author when he visited the temple in 1971.

congratulations. As soon as the student entered the Master's room and burst out with a loud bellowing "Mu," the Master swatted him with his fan. Immediately the student's face turned red with anger. Seeing this, the Master added with a gentle smile: "If you really understand that everything is Mu, why are you angry?" The student was not dull and caught his teacher's point. Mu must be lived in the stream of daily life flowing by us all the time and not stratified into an abstract concept by the understanding. When Mu is grasped as a concept and not a living reality, it has been lost. With a blink of the eyes we have missed seeing. A man may have a thorough intellectual understanding of the doctrine of emptiness, but if he gets angry when insulted, clamors for praise and fame, and feels upset when he does not get his way, he cannot be said to have realized emptiness. Mu is not so much an idea as it is a state of being. The man who lives in Mu may not be able to explain it, but if he can really demonstrate Mu in every phase of his day to day life he is an accomplished man of the Way.

The second step in Zen realization brings us from the void back into the world of actuality. We here realize that although everything is empty, still things are what they are. After the Zen master brings the student from the experience of nothingness in the first step back to empirical reality in the second, he tries in the third step to raise the mind of his student to the profound Middle Way (Jap.: *Chudo*) which goes beyond all dualistic concepts. This is the attainment of "the mind which clings neither to nothingness nor to actuality." It is the truth which lies beyond (and yet within) the realm of relativity, the unutterable, inexpressible truth transcendent over all dichotomies posited by the conditioned mind. This state is called in Japanese *shinku-myou*, the "truly non-existent but mysteriously existent." It is non-existent because all erroneous imaginings have been removed; it is existent because it is the permanent, abiding nature of all forms. Here everything is Mu, but we are still living here and now in this world of space and time where rivers flow and the sun shines afresh each day. We may catch it if we can, but we must not try to hold on to it for it will soon be gone.

The Middle Way is not only a philosophical concept in Zen Buddhism, but a practical one as well. In terms of practice the Middle Way teaches us to avoid all extremes of thought and action, to hold fast to the golden mean between excess and deficiency. In the practice of Buddhism to exceed may be just as bad as to fall short. We must not tune our strings too tight or too loose, for in neither case can we play music on our lutes. It is only when the strings are at a median degree of tautness, tense yet flexible, that we can play upon them. Similarly, in cultivating the Way we should avoid blind valor and excess of zeal just as much as lethargy. If we are excessively zealous, then it becomes too easy to lose heart when we meet difficulties and abandon the practice; if we are lazy, we will neglect to practice and go nowhere at all. As a practical concept Mu must also be carefully interpreted in the light of the Middle Way. On the one hand, we should avoid the extreme of quietism, using the nothingness of things as a passageway to escape from the world of human affairs into the dream of a blissful beyond. On the other hand, we should avoid the even more dangerous extreme of nihilism, asserting that since everything is void anything is permissible. Everything may be Mu, but that does not mean that a person can be justified in doing whatever he wants to. As long as we live in this world we must conform to the basic laws which give it structure, the principles of ethics and social harmony, even when we see that the world together with its laws are not final actualities in themselves.

Even the Enlightened Ones do not act contrary to the laws which they have transcended; how much more do these laws apply to the unenlightened. We must accept the world on its own terms and attempt to transform it from within. This is the path of the Bodhisattva who, though abiding inwardly in the tranquil bliss of the void, shows himself outwardly in this world of tribulation to teach and transform living beings. He may appear even as an ordinary man, inconspicuous amidst the crowd, laughing the laughter of the world and weeping with its sorrows, working ceaselessly through his charity and compassion to lead all within the bonds of Saṃsāra to the peace of Nirvāṇa.

A Chinese Zen master once said: "Before a man studies Zen, to him mountains are mountains, and rivers are rivers; after he gets an insight into the truth of Zen through the instructions of a good master, mountains to him are not mountains, and rivers are not rivers; but after this, when he really attains to the abode of rest, mountains are once more mountains, and rivers are rivers." What is the meaning of this? The first sentence expresses the viewpoint of the unenlightened man, the common understanding which views things in terms of false thinking. This requires no explanation, for it is a viewpoint with which we are all familiar. The second sentence is more difficult. Why does he say that the mountain is not a mountain, the river is not a river? Let us understand it this way: What is a mountain? A mountain is a combination of many rocks, trees and plants which we group together under the name "mountain." Hence the mountain is not a mountain. Again, what is a river? A river is a combination of many drops of water rushing and flowing together, a combination which is constantly changing. There is no abiding entity, "river." Hence, the river is not a river. This is the meaning of the second sentence. In the third sentence the Master says that for the man who has fully realized Zen the mountain is once again a mountain and the river once again a river. Conceptually this

way of looking at things is indistinguishable from the viewpoint of common sense, but experientially, the vision of the
enlightened man is radically different from his vision before
enlightenment. Earlier when he looked at the mountain, he
viewed it with a discriminating mind. He saw it as high or low,
big or small, beautiful or ugly. His discriminating mind gave
rise to love and hate, attraction and repulsion. But after enlightenment he looks at things with utmost simplicity. He
sees the mountain as a mountain, not as high or low, the river
as a river, not as beautiful or ugly. He sees things without
distinction or comparison, merely reflecting them like a mirror
exactly as they are.

To many of us, life in this world is full of suffering. Zen
teaches that if we wish to end suffering we should learn to view
all things as Mu, as nothingness. Since the cause of our suffering is attachment, when we see that the objects of our attachment are fundamentally unreal, we find nothing to be attached
to. But, in turn, we should not become too fond of nothingness. If we become attached to nothingness, we will want only
to withdraw from life and from the great community of
mankind in which we are enmeshed. We must try to do our
best for the world. A wisdom devoid of compassion is only a
dry wisdom. What is required is a wisdom permeated with
compassion and overflowing in acts of charity, self-sacrifice and
love. And when in our efforts to transform the world we meet
with failure, we should not become disappointed. The important thing is to act to the best of our ability and to leave the
results to the great law of cause and effect. We should develop
what the *Diamond Sūtra* calls "a mind which does not abide
anywhere." Realizing that all forms are empty and void, that
whatever arises perishes, abandoning attachment to the fruits
of our action, we act with supreme relaxation. We act with the
effortless action the *Tao Te Ching* describes thus: "He does

nothing, but there is nothing he does not do." Even in meditation we should not become too attached to concepts, not
even to enlightenment, Nirvāṇa, or Buddhahood. The Zen
masters always teach their students not to seek Buddhahood,
for if they seek to become a Buddha, that Buddha will become
an obstacle to their meditation. When we seek Buddhahood as
an object outside ourselves, we fall into the dualism of subject
and object, and by their very nature subject and object can
never become one. But if we give up all discrimination, subject
and object will vanish of their own accord. Then we will see the
Buddha within. This Buddha is the original Suchness, the
Clear Light shining in the Void, the underlying unity of all
things. To realize it is to experience enlightenment.

METHOD OF PRACTICE

Mu can also be used as a meditation technique. This
method is practiced primarily in the Rinzai Zen tradition,
where the *koan* "Mu" is especially emphasized. The body is
kept straight, the hands together on the lap, with the thumbs
touching each other on top so as to make a circle. This circle
represents Mu, the moon and emptiness. During meditation
the mind is kept in a state of emptiness. The meditator meditates that he is Mu, that all beings are Mu, that everything is
Mu. Because all is Mu there is no separate identity. All men are
interrelated and interdependent, all extensions of each other.
Through this method of meditation we can realize the oneness
of all things. In this oneness we can discover our true Self and
learn to live in harmony with others and in unity with the
whole universe. Let us be with Mu, meditate on Mu and feel
Mu—nothing more or nothing less.

9

Three
Goals of Zen

Whenever we do something in our daily life, we set ourselves a goal which gives purpose to our activity and infuses it with meaning. The same holds true with our practice of Zen. There are many goals to the practice of Zen meditation, but three stand out as the most important. It is these which need to be examined.

The first goal is called in Japanese, *joriki*. *Jo* means concentration, and *riki* means power. Thus, *joriki* is the power of concentration which develops through the practice of meditation. Concentration is an integral part of the "triple training" recognized by Buddhism as essential to the attainment of enlightenment. The triple training consists of moral discipline (*śīla*), concentration (*samādhi*) and wisdom (*prajñā*). From the viewpoint of practice Zen stresses concentration rather than morality or wisdom. The reason the emphasis of Zen is so placed is because the practice of Zen presupposes moral discipline and results in the arising of wisdom. So the other two are, in a sense, already included in concentration. The power which accumulates through the concentration of the mind is *joriki*. This, accordingly, is the first goal of Zen.

The mind that has been disciplined through the practice of meditation becomes transformed into a reservoir of power. Amidst the vicissitudes of the external world, the concentrated mind abides strong, steadfast and unshakable. It does not, like the untrained mind, leap from thought to thought and from desire to desire, but remains ever poised in the equanimity of its own tranquil depths. The concentrated mind stands supreme over the environment pressing in upon us from without, and supreme again over the passions and emotions threatening from within. It does not succumb to the propensities of lust, anger, pride, envy and delusion, but controls, restrains, conquers and extinguishes these passions, thereby finding for itself the freedom of its own unconditioned nature.

Through concentration the mind may acquire many paranormal powers, such as clairvoyance, clairaudience, thought-projection and the like. These powers, though they are indeed rare, are not supernatural, but merely supernormal. They are, in fact, inherent in latent form in the mind of every man and require only exertion in meditation to come to manifestation. The Buddha possessed these powers to a superlative degree, but we can find them exemplified in a mild form in everyday life. Sometimes, for instance, we may be thinking about somebody we love while just at that moment that person is thinking about us. Several years ago I sat down to write a letter to a friend from whom I had not heard in a long time. At the same moment I began to write to him, he was writing a letter to me. Why did this happen? Because through its thought-waves, mind can communicate with mind even across great distances of space. Another example is found in the relationship between a mother and her child. When the child meets some injury far from home, the mother may not know, but she often will feel a certain uneasiness in her heart. Many Buddhist monks who have developed the power of meditation know events that are taking place in areas beyond the range of sense perception. Enlightened masters can read deep into the hearts of people even with a single glance. By the power of mind the Zen master can know everything that is taking place in the minds of his students and guide them in ways fitting their dispositions and stages of attainment.

The power of meditation even enables a person to transcend his environment. Once there was a Zen master who was walking in meditation in the garden of his monastery. As he walked his mind entered into a state of deep absorption, so deep that he stepped right into the lotus pond without noticing. He continued walking, entering deeper and deeper into meditation and deeper and deeper into the pond. Though the water rose up to his neck, he still did not pay any attention to it. Then a student came into the garden and saw his master neck deep in the pond. The student yelled in alarm, jumped into the water and lifted his master out. When the Master was out of the pool, the student said: "Did you not realize that you were walking in the pond and could have drowned?" The Master looked at the student, remarkably quiet, and replied: "Is that so? Is that so?" How could the Master walk in the water without feeling it to be water? Because he was in deep meditation. In such a state of consciousness he could have gone on into deeper water without any problem. Perhaps he could even have gone on until he was completely submerged without drowning!

When we enter into profound meditation, our mind becomes master of everything. Water and fire no longer threaten. As long as we make a distinction between fire and no-fire, then whenever fire comes close to us, we feel the heat and run away. But when, through deep meditation, we pass beyond such discriminations, then there is no fear of the heat at all. Thus, in India there are many yogis who can sit in meditation under the blazing Indian sun without feeling hot, and in China and Japan there are many Zen masters who can sit in meditation all night during a winter's snowfall without feeling cold. The picture of the Vietnamese monk, the Venerable Thich Quang-Duc, on the wall of our Center, reveals him sitting in meditation surrounded by flames. The fire consumes his robes and his entire body, yet he sits as calm and motionless as a rock. His inward state of mind is best described in the poem of an old Chinese Zen master:

> For the tranquillity of zazen, mountains and streams
>   are not necessary;
> When the mind is extinguished, fire feels cool of itself.

How is this possible? By *joriki*, the power of meditation.

There are four pairs of opposites that hold man in bondage: pleasure and pain, gain and loss, honor and dishonor, and praise and blame. When these eight worldly winds blow, men find themselves torn between them, running toward one of each pair and fleeing the other. But when the mind is poised in the tranquil state of meditation, it can remain steadfast like a mountain, even when subjected to all kinds of abuse. The Buddha had a lay disciple who often neglected his wife in order to go listen to the Buddha preach. This made his wife feel very lonely, and very angry. She was angry not only with her husband, but also with the Buddha. She believed that the Buddha was using some mystical power to steal her husband. One day, after her husband had come home late the night before, she went to the Buddha to speak her mind. She yelled at him and abused him with very harsh words. The Buddha sat listening quietly, without speaking. The disciples did not like to hear the Master addressed with such language and tried to push the woman away. The Buddha made them stop. The woman continued upbraiding the Buddha for a time and then left without saying good-bye. After she left, the disciples asked the Buddha why he did not answer her back. The Buddha said:

"Let me ask you first. If somebody were to offer you a pleasing gift, what would you do?"

"We would accept it, Lord."

"If somebody were to offer you a disagreeable gift, what would you do?"

"We would not accept it, Lord."

"If you did not accept it, what would become of it?"

"It would remain in the owner's hands."

The Buddha continued: "Now just that has happened with the woman who was here. She offered me a disagreeable gift, and I did not accept it. So that gift is still in her hands."

The second goal of Zen Buddhism is called in Japanese *kenshogodo*. *Kenshogodo* means seeing or realizing one's true nature, and the term is equivalent to *satori*, or enlightenment. To attain *kensho* is to realize the Buddha nature within ourselves, to see that there is no fundamental difference between the Buddha and our own innermost essence. *Kensho* involves not only self-realization, but realization of others also. When we realize that we cannot exist alone, that we do not exist in a state of isolation but in a state of interdependence, that is *kensho*. But there are many different degrees of *kensho*, ranging from a brief flash of insight into the realm of truth to complete and permanent realization of the Buddha Mind. The terminology used to describe *kensho* also differs greatly. It may be called the realization of the infinite Mind, of the oneness of all beings, of the non-differentiation of oneself and others, of subject and object, Nirvāṇa and Saṃsāra, etc. *Kensho* could also be described as the experience of the truth that "everything is one, the one is nothing (*mu*), and nothing is everything."

The attainment of *kensho* is especially emphasized by Rinzai Zen. According to Rinzai teaching, it is not sufficient merely to accept the truth that every living being has a Buddha nature. What one must do is realize that truth. To bring about this realization the Rinzai school has evolved a number of dynamic techniques, the most famous being the *mondo*, a short question and answer exchange between a master and a disciple, and the *koan*, a philosophical topic, word or phrase which cannot be solved intellectually and is therefore given to the Zen student to help him break through his conceptual mind to the realm beyond thought. A person who realizes his Buddha nature, Rinzai Zen asserts, also realizes the Buddha nature in every being. Through *kensho* one discovers that he and others are not different, that there is no distinction between him and the universe. He can then see that "he is an extension of others, and others are an extension of him; between them there is no difference." As long as we think in terms of ego-consciousness we are distinct beings. But when we throw off the tyranny of ego in a flash of *satori*, we see that we are, at root, one. When someone is happy, we are happy. When we are happy, they are happy. If we help someone, he is also helping us. Why? Because we are extensions of each other.

The egoless viewpoint taken by Zen goes contrary to the egocentric viewpoint of the Western mind. In the West everything is thought to center around the "I." Even when we write the first-person singular in English, we capitalize it. In the East, in Chinese or Japanese, when we write the first-person singular, we usually use a small letter which occupies only half the space of the other letters. This is because in the East we try to minimize the importance of the "I," or ego. Thus we find that Buddhism teaches the non-existence of an ego-principle

while Hinduism teaches the elimination of egotism by subor-
dinating the individual self to the Universal Self or Ātman.
Along the same lines we find that Oriental people are usually
very humble. When a rich man in the Orient invites a friend to
his home, even if he lives in a large, luxurious house, he still
asks his friend to come visit his "small hut." This shows a deep
humility which is badly needed in the West. Again, in Chinese
and Japanese, when a man writes a letter, he usually addresses
the recipient as *sensei*, a term of respect meaning teacher or
sometimes elder; if he writes a letter to a classmate, he might
refer to him as *gakukei*, elder brother in study. Do you know
why the Orientals refer to each other as *sensei,* or teacher?
Because everyone can teach us something. Every individual has
some special gift, whether of knowledge, of character or of
skill, which he can communicate to others. Therefore, we can
all be teachers of each other.

The mutual love and respect which flows from the discovery of the Buddha nature in every being is also a kind of
kensho. *Kensho* means not only self-realization, but the realization of oneness with others also. To share the happiness and
suffering of others is *kensho*, as well as to delight in their welfare
and work for their good. *Kensho* can be found in the sense of
oneness with another person, with the flowers in a garden, with
the rocks and leaves and moss, with the fish swimming in the
pond, with the clouds moving in the sky, with the realm of
nature as a whole. There are many different aspects and degrees
of *kensho*, but to explain this in human language is difficult, for
kensho transcends the limits of words. *Kensho* is also difficult to
describe because the experience of *kensho* is individual and
always momentary. Like thunder and lightning it comes and it
goes. It never returns in the same way twice. A Zen master,
through his meditation practice, may prolong his experience of
kensho until it embraces an extended period of his awareness,

but for common people, with monkey-minds, *kensho* comes in a flash and then disappears. To develop our *kensho* we must practice meditation; then when *kensho* becomes permanent, full and perfect, that is the state of Buddhahood.

The third and highest goal of Zen Buddhism is called *mujodo no taigen*, the actualization of the Supreme Way. The actualization of the Supreme Way is the realization of the truth of enlightenment in our everyday life. It is the fusion of the *satori* experience with our daily activities in so complete a manner that no distinction can be made between them. Working in the garden, cleaning house, washing the dishes, driving the car, all become so many expressions of Zen realization. At the beginning of the path Nirvāṇa seems very remote from the world of everyday experience, abiding serene and blissful in majestic solitude. But after enlightenment it is now seen that this very world is identical with Nirvāṇa and our life itself an unfolding of the flower of Buddhahood. While seclusion, renunciation, ascetic practices and long stretches of solitary meditation may have formed a part of the path during the stages leading up to attainment, once attainment is reached and perfected all these become superfluous. We now find:

> My daily activities are not different,
> Only I am naturally in harmony with them.
> Taking nothing, renouncing nothing,
> In every circumstance no hindrance, no conflict. . .
> Drawing water, carrying firewood,
> This is supernatural power, this marvelous activity.

When we attain the actualization of the Supreme Way, we come to realize that all things are perfect just as they are. As long as we live in a world of dualistic judgments—good and bad, right and wrong, high and low—we become trapped in the bonds of attachment and find ourselves torn between the conflicting impulses of love and hatred, attraction and repul-

The masters lead the newly ordained monks and nuns back to the zendo after the transmission of the precepts during the Great Ordination Service, July 1974.

sion. But when we cease to cherish discriminating thoughts, everything can be accepted just as it is. We see that every day is a good day, and every way is a good way. We become like a bird flying through the sky without any goal or any sense of direction. For him just the flying itself is the goal, and every direction is the right direction. The attitude of the Zen student is just like that—if he meditates and studies, that is good; if he works to fulfill his responsibilities, that also is good. When we have an open mind, everything can teach us a lesson; we can find all the wisdom we require in every blade of grass and particle of dust. In the *Amitābha Sūtra* the Buddha explains that in the Pure Land of Amita Buddha the singing birds, the flowing waters, the drifting clouds and the blossoming flowers all teach the Dharma of Enlightenment. If we have an awakened mind, it is not necessary to travel to the Pure Land to receive such instructions. Everything is a manifestation of the Dharmakāya, the Reality principle, and hence everything is an expression of the Buddhadharma. Our teachers are present on all sides. We need only open our eyes to see them and our ears to hear them. This very world is the world of Enlightenment, this very earth the Absolute Body of the Buddha. To stride upon this earth with love and reverence, to learn from everything we meet, to treat all with kindness and compassion, this is to actualize the Supreme Way.

The full actualization of the Supreme Way is found in the career of the Bodhisattva. The Bodhisattva is a being who has set out to win the fruit of Buddhahood in order to deliver all sentient beings. His life is a fusion of two great spiritual forces, wisdom and compassion. Through his wisdom the Bodhisattva sees into the emptiness of all phenomena and brings himself to the realization of the unconditioned permanent Reality, Suchness or the Void. But by reason of his compassion the Bodhisattva does not enter into final liberation, but remains behind in this world of tribulation in order to enlighten and emancipate his fellow beings. His life is an ever flowing stream of compassion, love, kindness and charity. He thinks nothing of his own benefit, but dedicates himself completely to the benefit of others. By working for the welfare of his fellows, the Bodhisattva can find Nirvāṇa right in the midst of this stream of transmigration. For him Saṃsāra, the ocean of birth and death, and Nirvāṇa, the ultimate bliss, are not different. There is even a Bodhisattva named Kṣitigarbha (Jap.: Jizō), who remains in hell to relieve the suffering of the beings reborn there, and he finds Nirvāṇa while dwelling in hell. So when we attain realization for ourselves, the true task of Zen is not yet completed but has really just begun. For we must seek to bring the bliss of Enlightenment to all. To follow the Bodhisattva way of enlightening others, this is to fully actualize the Supreme Way.

METHOD OF PRACTICE

Just as the truth of Zen can be found not only in meditation but in every activity, so meditation can be practiced not only when sitting quietly but also in the midst of action. One popular action-meditation is called *kinhin* in Japanese, which means "walking meditation." The student stands up and puts the right hand on the back of the left hand, with the thumb of the right hand between the left thumb and forefinger. Then both hands are folded across the chest. Keeping the body erect and the eyes cast down at the toes, the meditators walk slowly and rhythmically in single file. Walking meditation is very helpful between periods of sitting meditation. It aids the circulation in the legs and helps eliminate drowsiness of mind, which might result from a long sitting. Also, by practicing *kinhin* we learn to keep the mind in the meditative state even when we are active. The most important feature of this method is mindfulness. We should be mindful of our action, watching ourselves walk step by step without thinking about anything else. If we can meditate while walking, then we can develop meditation in all our daily activities—driving the car, washing the dishes or working in the garden.

10

Non-Attachment

One of the most important teachings of Zen Buddhism is non-attachment. The teaching of non-attachment may be easy to understand, but it is not easy to practice. Nevertheless, it is very essential to cultivate non-attachment if we are to live a serene and happy life in a world of constant change; for this reason it is introduced here.

Our world is a world of desire. Every living being comes forth from desire and endures as a combination of desires. We are born from the desire between our father and mother. Then, when we emerge into this world, we become infatuated with many things, and become ourselves well-springs of desire. Through desire we give rise to attachments. For every desire there is a corresponding attachment, namely, to the object of desire. For example, we are most conspicuously attached to our bodies. When someone threatens the body, we grow anxious and try to protect it. We relish physical comforts and the enjoyments of the senses. Thus, we are strongly attached to the body. But if we consider this attachment, we will see that it is a potential source of suffering. For the body is constantly changing. We wish we could remain alive forever, but moment after moment the body is passing from youth to old age, from life to death. We may be happy while we are young and strong, but when we contemplate sickness, old age and the ever present threat of death, anxiety overwhelms us. Thus, we seek to elude the inevitable by evading the thought of it. The lust for life and the fear of death are forms of attachment.

We are attached not only to our bodies but also to our possessions. We continually weave a net of clinging around our clothes, our car, our house and our wealth. We loathe to part with these things and always try to accumulate more of them. We are also attached to memories concerning the past or anticipations of the future. Many people write diaries because they cannot part with their experiences, but wish to preserve them in such a form that they can always recollect them. When explorers climb a high mountain peak, what do they do? They leave their name on a rock or tree. When the astronauts landed on the moon, they left their footprints and the American flag. These attachments are based on the egocentric point of view, with its offspring, the notions of "me" and "mine." Even spiritual experiences may become objects of attachment. Through meditation we may gain some unusual experience or even *satori*; then we become attached to these attainments. This is another form of attachment. Zen Buddhism teaches us to extinguish attachment in order that we may discover the state of absolute freedom which is rightfully ours. The path to freedom is difficult to follow, but if we have sufficient determination, we can do it.

The Zen teaching of non-attachment is very similar to the teaching of Taoism. The *Tao Te Ching*, an ancient Taoist classic,

says: "When the sage walks, he leaves no footprints behind."
What does this mean? It does not mean that when the Taoist
sage goes for a walk one would not be able to find the imprints
of his feet on the ground. The sage is human like us, and so he
has footprints. What the statement means is that in his journey
through life the sage leaves no traces of desire and attachment
clinging to him as he lives from moment to moment. Life is
flowing, always changing, and the sage never looks back to the
moment which has just sped by, nor does he look forward to the
moment which lies ahead. Rather, he lives in the present,
flowing along in harmony with the rhythm of life, appreciating
each moment for what it is worth and allowing it to pass on
quickly to be replaced by the next. The Greek philosopher
Heraclitus said that nobody can step into the same river twice.
We may think that the river we step into tomorrow is the same
river we stepped into today, but this is just an illusion. The river
is always flowing along, so we can never step into the same
waters twice. Another saying famous in the West holds: "Nobody can say that today I live, and tomorrow I will live." In our
minds we may have plans not only for tomorrow but for next
year, and for ten years in the future, but no one can be certain
that he will even live through the night. Recognizing the
radical impermanence of life, Zen Buddhism suggests that we
should not be too strongly attached to life, for if we are, we will
find ourselves buffeted against the sharp rocks of change.
Instead of living in the past and future, we should learn to live
in the present as fully as possible. This moment, at least, we
are alive, while we cannot be sure we will be alive tomorrow.

The secret of non-attachment is revealed in the philosophy
of Chuang-Tzu, the great Taoist sage. According to Chuang-
Tzu, life and death are two sides of the same coin, so there is no
reason to be attached to life and afraid of death. As Chuang-Tzu
says in a poem:

There is the globe,
The foundation of my bodily existence.
It wears me out with work and duties,
It gives me rest in old age,
It gives me peace in death.
For the one who supplied me with what I needed
    in life,
Will also give me what I need in death.

When Chuang-Tzu's wife died, his friend the philosopher Hui Shih went to his house to console him and found him not weeping and wailing as one might expect, but laughing and singing. Asked how he could be so ungrateful to his wife, the sage replied: "When she had just died, I could not help being affected. Soon, however, I examined the matter from the very beginning. At the very beginning, she was not living, having no form, nor even substance. But somehow or other, there was then her substance, then her form and then her life. Now by a further change, she has died. The whole process is like the sequence of the four seasons—spring, summer, autumn and winter. While she is thus lying in the great mansion of the universe, for me to go about weeping and wailing would be to proclaim myself ignorant of the natural laws. Therefore I stop." From this story we learn that the key to happiness is non-attachment, and the secret of non-attachment is right understanding. If we cling to the desire for things to be permanent, then we will develop strong attachments, and because of attachment we will suffer. This is the second of the Four Noble Truths taught by the Buddha in the first sermon after his Enlightenment: "All suffering arises from desire." As a consequence, if we recognize rightly that all phenomena are subject to change and transformation, then there will be no room in our hearts for fear and worry. We can accept anything, even death, with a peaceful, cheerful mind. The accomplished Zen

man or woman can face all the vicissitudes of life and death
without fear.

There are some Zen masters who know the time of their
death several days in advance. When their time for departure
comes, they gather their disciples together, give them final
instructions and a *gāthā* embodying the essence of their teaching and then quietly pass away, often sitting in the lotus
posture. One Vietnamese Zen master named Tran-Nhan-Ton
left the following *gāthā* for his disciples at the time of his death:

> All things have no beginning;
> All things are without cessation;
> If you understand this,
> All the Buddhas are there.
> So how can there be any coming and going?

The spirit of non-attachment is beautifully illustrated by
the life of the Buddha. When he was still a prince, married to a
lovely wife and the heir to his father's throne, what did he do?
He renounced his family, wealth and power and fled to the
mountains to meditate upon the way to truth. After his Enlightenment, the Buddha continued to exhibit the attitude of
non-attachment. Whereas most of the founders of other religions have claimed themselves to be the way, the light and the
truth, the Buddha claimed to be the man who points the way.
The Buddha is the wayfarer, the supremely enlightened guide
along the path leading to the truth, but he does not claim to be
himself the path of the truth. This is a very humble attitude, is
it not? Since it is a man who shows the way, there can be many
ways which men may follow. Therefore we find a great deal of
freedom and tolerance in Buddhism. The path which is right
for one man may not be right for another. There are 84,000
Dharma-doors that lead into the inner chambers of the Awakened Mind, and every Buddhist is free to practice those
Dharma-doors he feels are best suited to himself. We find in the

same spirit that Buddhists are not too attached to their own particular beliefs, even when they accept them with deep faith. In this respect, they follow the advice of the Buddha, who urged his disciples not to become angry or upset when others spoke critically of his teaching and not to become elated when others spoke in praise of it, but to maintain an equal, open mind in the face of both criticism and praise. For forty-nine years the Buddha wandered over India preaching his doctrine and instructing disciples, yet on the last day of his life he could say: "In these forty-nine years I have not said a single word." Why did he say this? Because he did not want his disciples to become attached to his teaching. He wanted them to practice the teaching and realize the truth for themselves rather than grasp upon his own verbal and conceptual formulations of the truth. He compared his doctrine to a raft which is used to cross from this shore of ignorance and suffering to the other shore of Enlightenment and Nirvāṇa. The raft is to be used rather than carried around on the head, just as the Dharma is to be practiced and realized rather than merely studied.

In Japanese Buddhism a Buddhist monk is usually called *un shui*. *Un* means cloud and *shui* means water, so a monk is a "cloud and water" man. Why is he called so? Clouds are fleeting and insubstantial, and water is constantly flowing. So the Buddhist monk is to be like clouds and water, wandering from place to place to help and to teach people without abiding anywhere permanently. He has no attachment to anything and no property. In Theravāda Buddhism a monk owns just three robes, a bowl, a razor and some small utensils. The purpose of this is to eliminate attachment. The Buddhist sits loose and travels light. While we may feel that it is possible to own many things without being attached to them, still it is easier to be unattached with few possessions. Therefore, a Buddhist monk is not supposed to own more than what he needs. He is supposed to rise above all attachments, not only to his personal possessions, but to nation and family as well. A Buddhist monk does not think that only a particular group of people related to him by blood is his family or that a particular country is his nation. He regards all sentient beings as his family and every place as his home. He is a universal man devoted to the welfare and the happiness of the whole world.

The role of non-attachment in Zen Buddhism is very far-reaching. In fact, it may be said that the aim of Zen is to root out each and every point of attachment until there is not even a speck of dust left for the mind to grasp. This means that not only such coarse forms of attachment as the passions and desires must be left behind, but also the more subtle threads of intellectual attachment. Even such notions as Buddhahood, Nirvāṇa and Enlightenment must be pulverized and scattered to the winds until only the Void remains, and even that must be cast away. This is the meaning of the Middle Way—the Way that rises above the duality of "this" and "that." As long as one bears the concept of Nirvāṇa or Enlightenment in mind, that concept is a barrier to his meditation. For this reason some Zen masters teach their students: "When you meditate do not wish to become a Buddha." Why do they say this? Because if one wishes to become a Buddha, then he is attached to the notion of Buddhahood. He makes Buddhahood an object and himself a subject, thereby constructing a false dualism once again. We must let go of everything, high and low, exalted and debased, pure and impure, existent and non-existent, and the mind will become calm and pure by itself. From this calm, pure mind we can begin to cultivate the wisdom that will grow into Buddhahood. When we cease to discriminate between subject and object, the two become one and we find that from the beginning our very mind is the Buddha.

Cutting off desire is an important aim in Zen, and to this end, all Saṅgha members cut their hair. Here, head monk Bhikku Suhita shaves the head of Karuṇā Dharma before she takes the *śramaṇerika* vows; other monks lead the lay followers in chanting: "As I cut off my hair, I wish that all sentient beings will cut off their attachments and desires and attain Buddhahood."

All men seek happiness. It is a universal trait of human nature. But men differ very much in their views about how happiness is to be achieved. One Vietnamese Buddhist writer compares happiness to a butterfly. He says: "Happiness is something very beautiful, just like a butterfly. On warm summer days the butterfly darts back and forth above the green grass and the colorful flowers, looking very beautiful. But one must not try to catch it, for when the butterfly is caught in the hand, it becomes no more than an insect." This means that we should let happiness come and go just like the butterfly. When it comes, we should just enjoy it and not try to grasp after it. And when it goes, we should watch it go calmly and peacefully; then it will come back again. If we try to grasp happiness and hold on to it forever, it will die in our hands. We must let its beauty come and go and enjoy it while it lasts. That is the way of life and the meaning of life too. This is the way of non-attachment.

This concept of non-attachment in Zen Buddhism is revealed in a short poem by a Vietnamese Zen master:

> Swallows fly in the sky,
> The water reflects their image.
> The swallows leave no traces,
> Nor does the water retain their image.

METHOD OF PRACTICE

A common method to help the student lessen his attachments is the koan method of Rinzai Zen. The *koan* is a philosophical topic given to a Zen student for meditation by the Zen master. It may consist of a single word, a phrase, a sentence or a short passage. A most famous *koan* is called "the sound of one hand clapping." Everybody knows what the sound of two hands clapping is like, but what is the sound of one hand clapping? That is the *koan*. The student meditates on it until he can hear the sound of one hand clapping. Many of us have heard the sound of silence. If we can hear that sound, then we can hear the sound of one hand clapping also. This *koan* does not stop with hearing or not hearing, but goes further. If we can hear the sound of one hand, why can we hear it, and how can we hear it? If not, why not? Where does the sound come from, and where does it go? What is the nature of the sound, and what is the nature of hearing? If this *koan* is solved, the meditator may consider that he has experienced *kensho*.

11

Every Day is a Good Day

For Zen practice to be meaningful, it must encompass and permeate the entire life. All Zen schools, especially Soto Zen, emphasize the fusion of Zen experience with everyday life. People sometimes believe that Zen meditation is something very remote from the ordinary concerns of life. They think that to practice Zen they must give up their daily routines, withdraw from life and seclude themselves in mountain solitude. This idea is not completely wrong. Our minds are often like wild monkeys, and to discipline the monkey-mind it is helpful to have a quiet place, for a time, where one can practice undisturbed. But this is only one aspect of Zen, and not the highest aspect at that. Zen also places great emphasis on this life and this world. For the Supreme Way is all-embracing, excludes nothing and rejects nothing. To actualize the Supreme Way it is necessary to fuse one's meditation with the circumstances of everyday life, otherwise meditation is useless.

A few years ago, on the way from San Francisco to Los
Angeles, I stayed overnight at the Zen Mountain Center at
Tassajara. That evening I gave a lecture. After the lecture some
of the students came to talk with me. I asked them how long
they planned to stay and practice at the mountain center. Some
planned to remain all their lives as monks and nuns, but most
intended to leave after six months or a year. Then I asked:
"After you practice six months or a year, then what are you
going to do?" They all agreed they would return home to live
ordinary lives and introduce the discipline they had learned to
their friends, relatives and acquaintances, so these could obtain
the same benefits through Zen that they themselves experienced in the mountain retreat. That is the way of Zen. A
person can devote his whole life to practicing Zen in the
mountains or the monastery if he wishes. He can join the
Saṅgha community as a monk or a nun to practice, teach and
spread the Dharma to benefit others. But he can also remain
in normal life, cultivating himself while at the same time
fulfilling his duties at home and in the community. The latter
is very important. By practicing in a quiet place one learns
how to discipline the mind, and one may attain *satori,* or
enlightenment. After the attainment of *satori* or the achievement of some degree of mental discipline, the Zen adept
should teach others by showing them the way he himself has
followed. This practice is one of the Bodhisattva's Great Vows:
"However innumerable sentient beings may be, I vow to save
them all."

Our center has purchased an adjacent house to develop
into a Buddhist monastery. The monastery will not only be for
monks and nuns, who are devoting themselves to the practice
and teaching of Buddhism full time, but also for others who
wish to stay for a limited period, a week or a few months or a
year, to train in Zen practice and the Buddhist way of life. If a

person wishes to stay and practice, that is very good. But if he wishes to return home to fulfill his duties and pursue his work, that also is very good. These people who return home will, it is hoped, bring the experiences they gain in the training period at the monastery to bear upon their daily lives. The purpose of the training period or retreat is centered around this idea. Perhaps for this reason in Thailand it is customary for every young man to become a monk and practice in a monastery for a short period of time.

The fusion of Zen Buddhism with everyday life is the central theme of the Soto school of Zen. Dogen Zenji, the founder of Soto Zen in Japan, said: "The religious observances for each day express our gratitude towards the Patriarch." This means that if we want to contact the Patriarch, a Bodhisattva, or the Buddha, or if we want to attain enlightenment for ourself, the observance of daily life as the vehicle of our practice is very necessary. The Buddha always emphasized that enlightenment can be attained not only when sitting in meditation, but when engaged in any kind of activity—walking, standing or reclining. We cannot sit in meditation twenty-four hours a day. Sometimes we must work, sit or rest. A person who is trying to attain enlightenment must meditate not only when sitting but also during his daily activities. Keeping the mind under control, concentrating on the object, being mindful of what he is doing, seeking the significance of life in daily activity; that is the method of Zen.

Following this method from moment to moment can lead to enlightenment right in the midst of daily routine. Hui-Neng was the Sixth Patriarch in the history of Zen Buddhism. How did he reach enlightenment? He was not an educated man. He also did not have much time to dedicate to sitting in meditation. Before he became Patriarch he was always too busy working to serve more than five hundred monks in the monastery—cooking rice, carrying water, collecting firewood, taking care of the garden, etc. But he always kept his mind under control no matter what he was doing. In this way he meditated, and in this way had a deep enlightenment, so deep that the Fifth Patriarch chose him as his successor over more erudite Shen-Hsiu.

In the West, knowledge is considered a key virtue and the rational mind the peak of man's development. But this is not so in Zen Buddhism. In Zen, actions speak louder than words. Doing is more important than knowing, and knowledge which cannot be translated into action is of little worth. We may know of a beautiful mountain, but unless we get into the car and drive, we will never reach the mountain. With enlightenment it is the same way. Many people, especially in the West, try to intellectualize the state of enlightenment. But enlightenment cannot be realized through the intellect, but only through practice. To become enlightened it does not avail one to read many books, attend many lectures and study many source materials. These may help get the feet on the path, but once the feet are on the path the rest depends upon the practice. If we cultivate ourselves, then we will have the experience ourselves. It is only in this way that we can reach our goal, and there is nothing more the Buddha or the Zen master can do for us.

The practice of Zen should not be confined only to periods of sitting in meditation, but should be applied to all the activities of daily life. If we are diligent in cultivating the Way, we will find that every day is a good day. There are no bad days at all, not even Friday-the-thirteenth. Whether a day is good or bad depends upon the mind. By itself, the day is neither good nor bad. If we think that any particular day is bad, then we will make it bad, and many bad things will happen to us. But if we really believe that all days are good, then each day will be good,

The Master gives *teisho* (formal lecture on Zen) for students every Sunday morning. These lectures are followed by meditation and tea. For serious students, the Master plays the important role of guiding the disciples' growth toward enlightenment.

and many good things will come to us. Life is always changing, moving from this state to that, but there is nothing bad about change in itself. Change is our teacher. By opening ourselves up to the flow of life we can learn something new each day.

Every day becomes a lesson to us. Therefore, whether life is good or bad depends upon ourselves. The instrumental factor here is the mind. As a Western poet says, "The mind can make heaven of hell and can also make hell of heaven." Heaven and hell do not exist objectively outside ourselves, but as states of mind. If our mind is in the state of heaven, then we are in heaven right here and now. This is the reason the Tendai school of Buddhism says, "One moment of mind contains the three thousand worlds." Because the mind makes everything, our practice of meditation is not separate from our daily life, and our daily life is not separate from enlightenment. Enjoy life, understand it and experience it to the full. But let it come and go as it is—do not cling to anything. If we stop and cling to anything, we cannot experience the whole of life, and then we cease to grow. So let the mind flow like water. Face life with a calm and quiet mind and everything in life will be calm and quiet.

This realization is well expressed in the following Zen poem.

> In the spring, hundreds of flowers;
> In autumn, a harvest moon,
> In the summer, a refreshing breeze;
> In winter, snow will accompany you.
> If useless things do not hang in your mind,
> Any season is a good season for you.

If asked what season we like most, some of us may say the spring, others may prefer the summer, others may prefer the remaining seasons. But the Zen man does not prefer any season. The reason is that he loves all of them: to him every season is good. In spring there are many beautiful flowers to look at. Enjoy them, Zen says, but do not cling to them. For if we cling to them, when they bloom in the spring we may be happy, but when they fade in the fall we will become sad. The man who practices Zen loves every season. He can find something enjoyable in each of them. In spring there are the flowers, in summer the cool breeze, in autumn the clear, crisp air and the harvest moon and in the winter the beauty of the snow. Each season has its unique beauty. To practice Zen is to open the mind so that all of them may be enjoyed. When each season comes, we ought to enjoy it; when it goes, we should let it go and open our mind to the next season.

If we are attached to nothing, then every day is a good day, but if we have attachments, then even an enjoyable day can become unpleasant. A story may help to illustrate this. A friend of mine from Vietnam who came here to study, dropped by to visit me after completing his program. We arranged to go to San Diego to see the San Diego Zoo. My friend not only wanted to see the zoo himself, but also wanted to take pictures of the animals to show to his friends when he returned to Vietnam. My part was to drive from Los Angeles to San Diego. My friend is a very careful man, and I am too. Before I go somewhere I usually check to see if I have forgotten anything. So when we got into the car, I asked my friend: "Do we have everything we need with us?" He checked and said yes, and I began to drive. After I had driven about thirty minutes, my friend, looking at the beautiful sky, suddenly remembered that he had forgotten his camera at my place. He became upset, so I asked him if he would like me to drive him back to Los Angeles to get the camera. He looked at his watch and said: "Maybe it's too late to go back now." I agreed, and we drove on. We arrived at San Diego about mid-day. After lunch we went to the zoo to look at the many wild animals, birds, fishes and snakes. But each time we saw something strange or interesting my friend would say: "I wish I had my camera with me." Over and over again he kept on saying this, until I could only say to him: "Shall we drive back to Los Angeles to get the camera?"

The library of the College of Oriental Studies provides students with resource materials for an extensive academic study of Buddhism. Over 10,000 volumes in Japanese, Chinese, Korean, Pali, Sanskrit, Tibetan and English are available, including a vast collection of Buddhist scriptures with complete editions of the Tripiṭaka in several languages.

He looked at his watch again and said: "It is too late." At that moment, he realized that his attachment to the camera was spoiling our day, and so from then on he forgot about the camera, relaxed, and we both enjoyed the zoo very much for the rest of the day.

In ordinary life every person thinks about his plans for the future, maybe one year ahead, or ten years or twenty years. To have a plan is to have a purpose in life, and that is good. Man differs from the other animals because he can learn from the experience of the past, make a plan in the present and set up a goal for the future. We should all have plans, but at the same time we should remember to live in the present, not in the future or in the past. We should do what we like to do in the present and let the future take care of itself.

Of course, in acting in the present we should take stock of the consequences of our actions for the future; for what is the future now will someday become the present, and we will have to face those consequences. Zen Buddhism, therefore, always suggests to us: "Do wholeheartedly what should be done today. Do not put off until tomorrow what can be done today." Many times we think: "I worked very hard today, so today I will not meditate. Tomorrow I will meditate longer." If that is the case, did we keep the promise? Did we meditate longer the next day? I am not so sure. One should always try his best to finish what he can today rather than wait until tomorrow. If he puts off until tomorrow what he should do today, then he has to think about it and bear it in mind. If we want a free and restful mind, we should do what we can today rather than wait until tomorrow. By this practice we can go to bed with a peaceful mind. Nothing will bother us very much, either at night or during the day, because we keep our mind empty of useless things. The saying "empty mind is Zen mind" helps a great deal. It is a good way to live, and a healthy way too, because if we keep our minds calm and quiet, our life will be more peaceful, and we will be less racked by tension and worry. The reason people are so nervous and worried these days is because they let external things dominate them all the time. If they can master their minds, nothing can bother them. They will be in a peaceful state of mind in any place and at any time. Some may think it is too difficult to control the mind. It is true the mind is often like a monkey, but with diligence the monkey can be tamed. The Buddhas, Bodhisattvas, Patriarchs and Zen masters and countless laymen and laywomen did it. So why not us?

The Soto Zen masters teach their students: "Meditate on no thought. Just sit in meditation thinking of nothing." If the students complain that their minds are too filled with thoughts, the master replies: "If any thoughts arise in your

The International Buddhist Meditation Center is composed of a Zendo (right) and student living quarters (left) for Zen practitioners.

mind, just forget about them. Do not pay attention to them, and do not create second thoughts. Everything comes, and everything will go, but you just sit still in meditation." This method is called *shikan-taza*. If we apply this method during the period of meditation, nothing will bother or disturb us. Thoughts, the environment and the atmosphere cannot ruffle our mind. And if we apply this same concept to our daily life, the vicissitudes and problems of the external world will no longer sway us. As the Vietnamese Zen Master Van-Hanh says in a poem:

> Our life is a simple gleam which comes and is gone,
> As springtime offers blossoms to fade in the fall.
> Earthly flourish and decline, O friends, do not fear at all.
> They are but a drop of dew on the grass of morn!

Master the mind, and anything that happens can be a lesson from which we can fathom the meaning of life. With a calm mind, we can be peaceful and happy even in the midst of chaos and trouble. To develop a calm mind, it is important to sit in meditation, but for Zen the calm mind that results from sitting in meditation should be applied to all our daily activities. It is easy to develop a calm mind sitting on a comfortable pillow before the Buddha altar or at the Zen Center. But it is more difficult, and therefore of greater value, to meditate in the hustle and bustle of action or under disturbing circumstances. In the history of Zen there have been many masters who attained enlightenment while collecting firewood, carrying water, sweeping the ground, gardening and washing dishes. So why cannot we achieve the same experience while writing, typing, driving, working, etc.? If we concentrate and are mindful of what we are doing, it is not impossible. In fact, it is the barriers that make our wisdom grow. The Buddha himself faced many obstacles before he became enlightened, but by struggling over them he arrived at the perfection of wisdom. We can do the same if we only put forth the effort.

According to Buddhist philosophy, our store-consciousness collects and retains seeds, or karmic residues, of all our actions, words and thoughts. If our actions, words and thoughts are good, then gradually our store-consciousness will become pure and clean. On the other hand, if we commit evil through our actions, words and thoughts, then our store-consciousness will remain in the darkness of delusion. On these grounds, we should purify our minds and train ourselves to maintain mindful awareness in all our daily activities. In this way each moment can become an opportunity for us to cultivate ourselves and realize our true nature. This is the meaning of *mujodo no taigen*, the actualization of the Supreme Way, which is the main emphasis of Zen and its highest attainment. If we like this idea, why not put it into practice? It is not so far away. We can do it right in our daily life.

METHOD OF PRACTICE

In Soto Zen the most common method of practice is *shikan-taza*, or no-mind meditation. The student sits quietly with his face to the wall and meditates inwardly with no thought in his mind. But Soto Zen also emphasizes meditation in daily life. One very pleasant practice is walking meditation in a garden. While walking in *kinhin*, the meditator should walk quietly with his five sense organs open and his mind ready to receive and become one with everything in nature. If his eyes see the blue sky, beautiful flowers and colorful fish in the pond, his ears hear the water fall and the birds sing, his nose breathes in the fresh air, but his mind still remains aware and mindful of what he is doing, that is good. This method gives an experience of unity between oneself and nature. When we experience that we and everything in the universe are not different, that we are a part of everything and everything is within us, in other words, if we realize the oneness of everything, that is *satori*. If we wish to experience *satori*, we may. All we have to do is practice.

12

Self-Power
and Other-Power

Zen Buddhism emphasizes man's ability to develop himself
through his own inner strength and states that by his own
determination and constant practice he can attain the state of
enlightenment and spiritual perfection known as Buddhahood. This reliance upon one's own effort as the way to enlightenment is known as "self-power," and the philosophy of
self-power forms the basis for practice in both the Rinzai and
Soto schools of Zen. However, Buddhism includes not only
the conception of self-power, but also the conception of an
"other-power," the compassionate power radiating from the
heart of Amita Buddha, the glorified Buddha of the Great
Vehicle. The philosophy of the "other-power" provides the
central conception of Pure Land Buddhism, a devotional form
of Buddhism which flourished in China, Vietnam, Korea and
Japan. But the concept of the other-power is not altogether
foreign to Zen. In Zen Buddhism there have been attempts to

fuse the concepts of self-power and other-power into a synthetic whole, and the result of this synthesis has been very fruitful for both theory and practice. The union of self-power and other-power runs throughout the practice of Zen in China and Vietnam, and while the two main Japanese Zen sects, Rinzai and Soto, tend to emphasize self-power exclusively, there is a third sect called Obaku Zen, which takes the fusion of the two powers as its basic method of cultivation. Some scholars, such as D. T. Suzuki, do not regard the reliance upon the "other-power" as authentic Zen, but this author's viewpoint is different. Any method which leads to the calming and purification of the mind and the realization of our true nature can be considered as Zen. Zen is the Japanese equivalent of the Sanskrit word *dhyāna*, "concentration" or "meditation." If the method of combining self-power and other-power as practiced in the syncretic Zen schools leads to the attainment of a concentrated mind and the opening of enlightenment, then that method is legitimate Zen.

The methods of self-power and other-power were both originally taught by Śākyamuni Buddha, the founder of Buddhism. According to the teaching of the Buddha, every living being has a Buddha nature. Therefore, it is within the potential of every man to realize that Buddha nature and to become enlightened. But to reach that state is a tremendously difficult task, calling for dauntless courage and unflinching will power. Thus, very few people are capable of reaching enlightenment by themselves; very few have the required spiritual qualification. For the majority of people it is necessary to rely upon the help of others, and here we find the germ of the "other-power" schools. It is as if a boat were wrecked while floating down a river. Those who are good swimmers would be able to save themselves, but what are they to do who cannot swim as well? They must call for help and rely upon a better swimmer to bring them to the safety of the riverbank. In other words, they must rely upon someone else to save them. Similarly, while we all have the potential to become Buddhas, very few can accomplish Buddhahood through their own unaided striving. Most must rely upon the help of others to reach the safe shore of enlightenment. In Obaku Zen and the Pure Land schools, practitioners rely upon the compassionate power of Amita Buddha. This may sound rather remote from orthodox Zen, but if we consider the matter carefully, we will find that the difference between Obaku Zen and Pure Land Buddhism on the one hand, and the Rinzai and Soto Zen schools on the other, is only a difference of degree, not of kind. Practice in Rinzai and Soto requires the Master to teach the student how to sit, how to discipline his mind, how to work with the *koan* or practice *shikan-taza*, and he depends upon the wisdom and spiritual skill of the Master to guide him to enlightenment. Without the constant prodding of the Master, how many people would reach *satori*? True, the Zen master cannot give enlightenment, but still he stands as a hand reaching to the disciple from the "other shore," ever ready to extend to him whatever help he requires. Now if the Zen master is able to assist in the struggle to reach enlightenment, then how much more help can we expect from the Master who has reached Perfect Enlightenment, the Buddha? The Zen master can help because he has realized a certain amount of wisdom and compassion. And so the Buddha can provide us with inexhaustible help because he has reached the state of perfect wisdom and infinite compassion. Even the very existence of the path of self-power is in a sense due to the "other-power" of the Buddha. For it was the Buddha who in his compassion taught the path to enlightenment and thereby made that path accessible to mankind. The Buddha is the person who helps us by showing us the Way, and we are the persons who work and practice it by ourselves. That is a union of self-power and other-power. If the self-power and other-power work together to assist each other, then we can go anywhere, reach anywhere we wish. By fusing these two powers in our daily practice, we can enter the gates of enlightenment and abide in the city of Nirvāṇa.

According to the Buddha, there were in the past other Buddhas who were his predecessors, and there will be in the future other Buddhas who will be his successors. The Buddha who is the primary focus of devotion in the Pure Land schools and in Obaku Zen is a Buddha of the remote past called Amita Buddha. Many aeons ago, the story told by Sākyamuni Buddha goes, there lived a Bodhisattva named Dharmākara, who practiced the meditations of compassion and loving-kindness. In his meditation he saw that all living beings are subject to suffering, to the sorrows of birth, old age, illness and death. Witnessing this suffering aroused in him a great compassion, and out of this compassion he vowed that when he attained Buddhahood he would create a special paradise in the Western region where there would be no more suffering. Through the power of his vow he would enable any living being recollecting his name and calling upon his help to be reborn in the Western paradise. Since the Bodhisattva Dharmākara, after several long aeons of self-cultivation, did attain Perfect Enlightenment and become the Buddha Amita, this means that his Great Vow is now a reality. The paradise has been established and is accessible to all who with a mind of sincere faith take refuge in the compassion and grace of Amita Buddha.

The Western paradise is not, however, the final goal for the Pure Land Buddhist, not even for those who seek rebirth there. Rather, it is an intermediary abode where the most favorable conditions for self-cultivation have been set up and secured. While there are some men who by practicing can reach enlightenment in this world, many find difficult obstacles confronting them along the path. The necessity for work, the attractions of the senses, the threat of illness and infirmity and the gross entanglements of materiality all stand as barriers across our path. In the Western Paradise none of these barriers are present. Everything there is radiant, peaceful and beautiful. No defilements can be found, for all shines with purity. Therefore, the country of Amita Buddha is called the Pure Land. Those who are reborn into the Pure Land dwell in the midst of lotus flowers. They are always in the presence of Amita Buddha and the assemblies of Bodhisattvas presided over by the Bodhisattva Kwan-Yin, the embodiment of universal compassion. In the midst of these pure conditions it is easy to develop concentration and wisdom and attain Perfect Enlightenment.

The way to attain rebirth in the Western Paradise is by devotion to Amita Buddha. This devotion is expressed by reciting the sutras that teach about Amita, by chanting His Name, by meditating upon His Image and by calling to mind His Wisdom, Virtue and Compassion. Those who are capable of placing single-minded faith in the Great Vow of Amita will enter the Pure Land where they will meet all favorable conditions for practice and never again fall into this world of suffering. This way is called the "easy path" (Jap. *igyo*) in contrast to the "difficult path" (*nangyo*) of self-power. The practice of the "easy path" is very popular in China, Vietnam, Korea and Mongolia, and also in the Pure Land schools of Japan, the Jodoshu and the Jodoshinshu. Belief in the "other-power" of the Buddha also helps us to develop our self-power. Therefore, in the Far East a form of practice was developed by Mahāyāna Buddhists which combines formal meditation with the chanting of the Buddha's name. In this method the practitioners sit before an image of the Buddha and chant the Buddha's name, quietly and calmly, while at the same time meditating upon the Buddha image or an internalized visualization of the Buddha. As the mind deepens in meditation, a point is reached where subject and object become one. No longer is the Buddha the object and the meditator the subject, but the meditator becomes one with the Buddha. When this happens, this is the state of "One Mind Samādhi," and here there is no longer any distinction between Zen and Pure Land, self-power or other-power, wisdom or compassion, for all has become merged into the brightness of the Infinite Light.

According to a popular Buddhist belief, whenever a person aspires to become a Buddhist, a lotus-flower blossoms in the Pure Land. When a person becomes a Buddhist, this means that he is beginning to practice the way of wisdom, compassion and virtue, so by the operation of the law of cause and effect, in the perfect world created by the compassion of Amita Buddha, a lotus flower, the symbol of inner spiritual awakening, awaits his rebirth into the realm of spiritual perfection. The Western paradise is called the Pure Land because it is the land of purity, and all who are reborn there are pure. Everything in the Pure Land teaches the Dharma. Even the birds sing the songs of the Dharma, the rivers hum sutras as they go flowing by and flowers blossom in harmony with the blossoming of wisdom. In the Pure Land everything is a stepping stone on the way to Perfect Enlightenment.

This concept is similar to the teaching of Zen. In Zen we do not learn only from a book or teacher, but from everything, and we do not learn only in a temple or a meditation center, but everywhere. For Zen is experience itself, the truth of life as it is ever flowing by and encompassing us on all sides. So if we approach life with an open mind, everything can be our teacher. The way of Zen is not a withdrawal from life, but the

realization of truth in all the activities of everyday life. We can
learn from our fellow men, from the arts. This is why Zen
developed the cultivation of such arts as gardening, poetry,
painting, tea ceremony and flower arrangement—as expressions
of and keys to the attainment of enlightenment. Zen has even
found a vehicle in the martial arts. The first supporters of Zen
when it was introduced from China to Japan were the *samurai*,
the warrior class, who found in Zen's emphasis on self-control
and equanimity of mind a method of discipline conducive to
their own ends. Zen has also influenced the development of
techniques of self-defense like judo and karate. The principle
underlying these different applications of Zen is that any field
of activity can serve as a means for realizing the truth of Zen. In
the same way, according to the Pure Land teaching, everything
in the Paradise of Amita Buddha is a teacher of the Dharma.

There are three methods of meditation practiced in the

The tea ceremony, performed here by Ms. Toshiko Sato at the International
Buddhist Meditation Center, Los Angeles, reflects the simplicity, quiet-
ness, beauty and harmony of Zen.

combined Zen-Pure Land schools. The first is the chanting of
the Buddha's name. The second method is the meditation
upon the form of the Buddha. The follower chooses a particularly appealing image of the Buddha and begins by focusing
upon that image until he can picture it clearly for himself; then
he closes his eyes and tries to visualize the form of the Buddha
internally. The third method is to meditate upon the virtues of
the Buddha. The Buddha is the embodiment of perfect wisdom
and infinite compassion. Either one or both of these virtues
together may be taken as the subject of practice. If we choose
the compassion of the Buddha, we reflect that the Buddha's
compassion makes no distinction between subject and object
or between enemies and friends, but pours down upon all
equally. This compassion is different from ordinary love. Ordinary love works according to various discriminations: we
love ourselves, but not others; our relatives, but not strangers;
our friends, but not enemies. However, the compassion of the
Buddha extends equally to everyone. Like the Buddha, we
should extend our love and compassion outward to all alike, to
everyone everywhere, without making any distinctions. Again,
if we choose to meditate on the Buddha's wisdom, we imagine
the light of wisdom radiating from the figure of the Buddha
and growing larger and larger and brighter and brighter until it
merges with our own inner light. At this point we and the
Buddha become one. When this stage is reached, then this
world will become transformed into the Pure Land, this
Saṃsāra become Nirvāṇa, and all the bliss and purity of the
Western paradise become realized in the here and now of
everyday life. Here the Zen and Pure Land schools meet in that
common center from which they both emanate, the One Mind
of Buddha, which is our own true and permanent Essence of
Mind.

METHOD OF PRACTICE

So far the methods of meditation which have been described are used in the Rinzai and Soto schools of Zen, such as the awareness of breathing, the koan method, the practice of *shikan-taza*, etc. The combined Zen-Pure Land tradition, such as found in China and Vietnam and in the Obaku Zen sect in Japan have some different methods. Two of them were described in this chapter. The third practice, which is the most popular method in the Far East, and also the shortest and the easiest, is the chanting of Buddha's name. The devotee sits in the usual meditation posture, calms his mind and his breathing, closes his eyes lightly and then chants the Buddha's name. Of course he can chant the name of any Buddha or Bodhisattva which he may prefer, but in the Far East it is most usual to chant the name of Amita Buddha since he represents the infinite compassion of Buddhahood. The Chinese thus chant, "Namu A-mi-to Fou," the Japanese, "Namu A-mi-da Butsu" and the Vietnamese, "Namo A-di-da Phat." They all mean: "I pay homage to Amita Buddha." The chanter may practice by chanting loudly to the rhythm of the *mokkyō* ("wooden fish"), or he may chant silently to himself. Whichever is chosen, the important thing is to chant with one mind, concentrating upon the chanting and excluding all other thoughts from the mind. According to the common expression, "the fingers should move along the Buddhist beads, the mouth chant the Buddha's name, the eyes see the Buddha's image, and the mind meditate on the Buddha's virtues." This method may be practiced not only when sitting in meditation, but all the time in any activity. We practice it until our mind becomes perfectly calm and quiet and Amita Buddha is always with us. We practice it further until we and the Buddha become one, until there is no name to be chanted and no one to chant it. When this happens, this land and the Pure Land become interfused in a perfect harmony beyond the realm of perception and knowledge. Then we change this Saṃsāra into Nirvāṇa, this suffering world into the Blissful Land of the West, this world of impurity into the Pure Land. To experience this reality, one only needs to chant, "Namo Amita Buddha," in complete sincerity, mindfulness and faith.

13

One's Self and Others

The true indicator of the Buddhist life is not words, not knowledge, but action. To sit in meditation is important; to keep the mind calm, quiet and disciplined during meditation is necessary, but this is not the most difficult task. The most difficult task is to carry that disciplined mind into daily life. In Mahāyāna Buddhism, the Bodhisattva is like the lotus flower, which is raised from the mud, yet does not smell of the mud, blossoming beautifully and sweetly. He lives in daily life, but is not tainted by it as he aids all living beings. A Zen student must strive to be like the Bodhisattva. He may live the life of an ordinary person, but his mind is always under control and filled with wisdom and compassion for all life forms.

To attain the Bodhisattva mind, the most important step is to have true awareness of one's self and one's relationship to others. Man is unique in his capacity for self-awareness and self-control. This capacity for self-knowledge is what makes the human world the best of the six realms in which to work out enlightenment. Men and animals differ not only in their form of being, but also in their levels of consciousness. An animal only has consciousness of his surroundings, his external world. Man is more developed than that, for he not only has conscious awareness of his external world, but also conscious awareness of himself, of his whole being.

Therefore, the first step toward enlightenment is to know what the self is. Does it exist or not exist? Is it permanent or not permanent? According to Buddhist philosophy, the self is a living being with two characteristics: combination (*anatta*) and changeableness (*anicca*). Our body, our life, is a combination of four different elements: hardness, wetness, breath and warmth. We cannot continue to live if these elements separate, since what we label "our body" is comprised of and continued by these four physical elements in combination with each other.

However, our life does not consist only of a physical body, but of a mind as well. Therefore, Buddhist philosophy also brings us to another awareness—the mind. What is the mind? Is it an entity? Is it permanent? Does it have substance? According to Buddhist thought, the mind is composed of four different elements: conception, perception, volition and consciousness. The mind is not unique, it is not permanent, and it is not real. In other words, life continues to exist because the mind and the body are joined to each other. Body and mind are not real in themselves (*śūnyatā*)—they are a combination of many different elements. And, because they are a combination of many components, life is changeable. From the past to the present to the future—moment by moment life changes. Nothing is permanent in this world, including the mind and the body. Life is like the circle of light created by incense when it is twirled. When the movement is stopped, the circle automatically disappears. The movement of life is the same. A *gāthā* of the Diamond Sūtra states:

> All phenomena in this world are
> Like a dream, fantasy, bubbles, shadows;
> They are also like dew, thunder and lightning;
> One must understand life like that.

Life is changeable because life is a combination of many different elements. However, even though it is a combination of different elements and subject to change, we still exist at the present moment in this world. Therefore, the most important thing is for us to know ourselves, to be aware of ourselves. This self-awareness takes us beyond an ego-involved consciousness to a realization of the true self, of the self that does not change according to past, present and future, of the self that is always us, the True Self, the Buddha nature. A famous Rinzai *koan,* "What was your original face before you were born?" is frequently given by Zen masters to help their students to realize this original face, this nature. Since self-realization is the goal of Zen, primary emphasis is laid upon it, and most meditation is aimed toward this end.

How can we realize the self? How can we be with the True Self if our mind is wandering and thinking many different things, bothered by worry or happiness? To steady the mind, Buddhism proposes the method of meditation. Meditation is a technique to keep the mind calm, quiet and pure. During practice the meditator does not ask where is God or Buddha; he does not worry about what happened in the past or what will happen in the future. He does not pay attention to events in the external world. Such concerns are not important. What is important is to be with the self here and now. Zen Buddhism, particularly, introduces methods that bring conscious awareness of the self, realization of the self here and now.

During realization of the self, the meditator comes to understand that no one can exist alone in this world. No one. He needs someone with him. One island may exist in the ocean, but one man cannot exist alone. So, at the same time that a man has awareness of himself, he must have awareness of other people, and he must also be aware of the relationship between the two.

We cannot exist alone in this world. Physically we need each other. This need brings us close to one another, and we help each other. For example, because I cannot make clothes and other things I need for my existence, I need other people. Everybody needs others; all of us, all mankind, are helping each other. According to Buddhist philosophy, life is a process of giving and receiving. Sentient beings are reborn to work out their karma, to receive help from others and at the same time to fulfill their part in helping others. Therefore, life is a process of giving and receiving: physically, spiritually and emotionally. Nevertheless, in giving we must remember one thing: we should not make any distinction between giver and receiver. If we think of ourselves as giving and someone else as receiving, then we will give rise to a sense of pride and expectation. From these arise all the problems with which mankind is familiar. In giving there should be no concept of a giver, a gift and a receiver. This attitude is expressed by the Buddhist term *śūnyatā* (Mu), which means emptiness or nothingness. At the same time that we give or receive, we should be aware thet nothing is given or received. The saying "non-giving and non-receiving of gifts" describes this attitude. To make the receiver happy we must give without thinking that we are giving favor. We must not place ourselves in a higher position and look down upon others as if they were lower than we are. In other words, we must give with a humble and compassionate attitude.

A key virtue of Buddhism is humility. To be humble is to avoid placing oneself above other people. A Vietnamese Zen Master once taught his disciples: "I am not necessarily a saint or a sage, and you are not necessarily a common man." From the Buddhist point of view, everyone is a human being, and because we are all human, we all have our weak points as well as our strong points. Nobody short of a Buddha, a completely Enlightened One, can be considered perfect. If we recognize that we are not yet perfect, then we cannot expect others to be more perfect than we are ourselves. This recognition creates better relations between men. To be aware that we are not yet perfect will not only make us more humble towards one another, but also more respectful and tolerant. For example, in a marriage relationship often the husband and wife expect their partner to be perfect. As a result, when they become aware of each other's shortcomings, they become disillusioned and unhappy. However, if they recognize that they themselves are imperfect, they will not place such heavy demands on each other and will be able to respect, tolerate and love each other more. Tolerance is a key factor in interpersonal relationships.

Every action we take, every word we speak causes a reaction in people around us. For example, if we feel anger, when others see us, they also share that anger with us. And when they see us happy, then they also share the happiness with us. We share not only our physical life and our material goods with each other; we share spiritual and emotional characteristics as well. Such is the act of relating between oneself and another. Because we are all related to each other, none of us is an island; all of us are a part of the whole. Men are not separate. The separation between oneself and another is not real. Our ego-consciousness and our illusion create the separateness. If we see through this ego-centricity and this illusion, then we see that we are not really different. Buddhist philosophy, as well as

Hinduism, always describes it this way: "You are my extension and I am your extension." Therefore, because everyone is our extension, when we intend to hurt someone, at that time we hurt ourselves. Likewise, because we are their extension, when they intend to harm us, they harm themselves as well.

Buddhism recognizes that all men and all living beings are interdependent. Though their bodies and minds are different, they are still interrelated. Since they are interrelated, they are not separate. We are all different facets of the same reality, different parts of the one whole, just as the numerous waves rising and falling in the ocean are interrelated transformations of the one ocean. Because we are all so inseparably bound together in the vast ocean of existence, Buddhism suggests that we should love one another. We must shift our sense of identity away from the narrow, constrictive ego-consciousness to the all-embracing universal consciousness. We must learn to see each other as extensions of the same reality. Then we can live together in the world as friends and brothers, and this world of hatred and suffering will be changed into an abode of peacefulness and bliss. This samsaric world will be transformed into Nirvāṇa.

The Buddhist tries to develop in himself a universal consciousness and non-discriminatory love during both sitting meditation and daily activities. To express this compassion, Buddhists remind themselves of the Bodhisattva vow: "Sentient beings are innumerable; I vow to save them all."

Why do people marry? Why do people need friends? When people are alone, they become very lonely, so they marry to have companionship between themselves and their beloved. Men and women need friends to provide companionship. But the problem lies here. We always recognize the closer relationship, but not the one farther off. We see that we need a friend, but at the same time we feel that we do not need those persons we do not consider to be friends. We may try our best to protect our friend, but at the same time, we may try to harm those we do not view in the same way—our enemies. However, friend and enemy are like yang and yin. Yang cannot exist without yin, and yin cannot exist without yang, just as male and female are inseparable. Friend and enemy are the same. Who makes a person become the friend or the enemy? We ourselves. If we change our attitudes toward another, if we are kind to another, then the other, even if he is now our enemy, will change his attitude and gradually become our friend. Likewise, if we are not kind to a person, even if he is our best friend, he will eventually change into an enemy. We must recognize that friend and enemy are merely different degrees of relationship between two persons and that we are the ones who make it so.

When the United States government considered the government of the People's Republic of China to be its enemy, then everything there was the enemy. Now that the relationship between the two countries is improving, people of both countries are beginning to view each other differently. We are no longer the enemies we were. During World War II the United States and Japan viewed each other as terrible enemies, but now they are close allies. Our relationships with others are caused by our attitudes and are easily changed. Living in this world in relationship with each other, we have to recognize that there are always two opposite elements: good and bad, friend and enemy, life and death, happiness and sorrow, yang and yin. At the same time, we must remember that these opposites are merely concepts, reflections of our attitudes. In reality they do not exist; there is no distinction. The thing to realize here is that all men are to some degree the same and to some degree different, and this recognition may help us to progress and to help others progress.

As mentioned, each of us lives in this world interrelated to each other. Also, each individual needs a companion. Companionship exists not only between men, but also between men and animals and men and nature. At home there are friends and relatives. Also, many people have animals—dogs, cats, fish, birds, turtles—some may even have a snake or more unusual pet. Keeping a pet helps to fulfill the need for companionship that is necessary not only with other people, but with animals and nature as well. In order to keep those relationships and to improve them, Buddhism suggests that we must understand the other's position, that we must develop a mutual understanding; that is the first important step.

In order to keep a good relationship between ourselves and other people, we must respect the other. This is the second step. When we meet each other, it is a Buddhist tradition to join our hands together and to bow and pay respect to each other. This bow reminds us that we respect each other because we are all destined to become Buddhas in the future. If we respect others, then they will respect and love us.

The third step which insures better relations with others is honesty. We must be honest both with ourselves and with others. By doing so, mutual understanding and mutual respect arise. Honesty with oneself and others will improve relationships between men, between oneself and other people.

Perhaps the most basic and yet most complex relationship is that of the family. The Western family tradition differs from the Oriental tradition. Western tradition places more emphasis on the individual, while the Oriental tradition places more emphasis on the family and the country. If the Western way is individualism, the Eastern way is nationalism, or maybe "familyism."

It is the family relationship which remains the most important of all relationships. The Buddha, recognizing this fundamental truth, suggested practical duties for parents and children to help build good family relationships. He taught that children would grow into mature, happy adults if parents fulfilled five basic duties to their children: (1) to restrain them from evil; (2) to encourage them to do good; (3) to train them for a profession; (4) to arrange a suitable marriage; (5) to hand over their inheritance to them at the proper time. In the Buddhist and Oriental traditions, as the parents grow old they give all their properties to their children.

The children also have five guides to follow: (1) to support their parents; (2) to perform their parents' duties if the parents cannot fulfill them; (3) to keep the family traditions; (4) to be worthy of the family inheritance; (5) to offer alms in honor of their parents and ancestors. Because Buddhist monks are very busy teaching and practicing, the laymen offer alms to them such as food. Sometimes the lay people do so to gain spiritual benefits for themselves, but usually it is to honor their parents, and such an offering done in true filial piety is very beneficial to everyone.

In Oriental traditions the children are supported by their parents when they are young, but when the parents grow older and stop working they need support from their children; such a custom keeps a close continuing relationship between parent and child. Not only do children remain close to their immediate parents, but to their grandparents—those who are still alive as well as those who have died. The family has an awareness of tradition which is not only present but past, since it includes those members of the family who have already died. This respect for family traditions forms the basis of ancestor worship in Oriental countries.

The Buddha also provided practical advice to people who marry. A man was admonished to perform the following duties to his wife: (1) to be courteous to her; (2) not to despise or belittle her; (3) to be faithful to her; (4) to hand over authority to her; (5) to provide her with adornment. A husband wishes his wife to look beautiful, but she cannot be beautiful if she does not feel beautiful. If the husband gives her adornments and gifts, she will feel happy, and when she is happy, she will be beautiful and he will be happy also. Buddhist marriage ceremonies usually include an explanation of these obligations of a husband to his wife, as well as five reciprocal obligations of the wife to her husband. The wife is told: (1) to perform her duties well; (2) to be hospitable to relations; (3) to be faithful to her husband; (4) to protect what he brings; (5) to be skilled in discharging her duties, that is, to be skilled as a wife and mother and in maintaining the household.

Although the duties outlined above may seem dated to Western society, they are based upon mutual respect and consideration and are still good advice for modern families. One can see in the husband's duties the germ of the women's liberation movement, and in the parent/child duties mutual love and caring.

Just as one man cannot exist alone in this world, one family cannot exist alone in this world. The family is part of the community, the community part of society and the society part of mankind. The Buddhist tradition realizes the oneness of human society, since one family cannot exist alone, one city cannot exist alone, one country cannot exist alone. All of us help each other and are related to each other. In Buddhist thinking, if we want to have world peace, we must have peace in our own minds first. If we want society to be harmonious and happy, we must develop a calm mind, a quiet mind, and improve ourselves first.

In the West many people who want peace believe they must fight, because peace, according to them, should be an honorable and a winning peace. Build up power, they argue, and we build up peace. This may be one method, but there are many methods. If we follow the Buddhist way, if we want to have peace, we must first have peace in our mind, in our life. When our mind, our life, our self is at peace, we influence others to develop peaceful minds, peaceful families and peaceful societies, and we have lasting peace.

Some countries achieve independence by fighting, by killing, by war, but some countries achieve independence not by killing, not by war, but by nonviolence. Gandhi and Nehru in India, Sucarno in Indonesia and Ho Chi Minh in Vietnam were very similar, but they applied different techniques for the same desired results. Ho Chi Minh wanted his country to be independent. Since he felt he had to fight, he fought with the French. Then he continued to fight with the Japanese, and then with others. The war continued for more than thirty-five years. How many people died? How much property and land was destroyed? At the same time, Gandhi and Nehru's independence movement was nonviolent. By this method they achieved independence without bloodshed, and in a shorter period of time. It would be good if all the world could follow the same method. Of course, everybody wants to protect himself, his family, his property, his country, but there are many different ways to do so. If we use the technique of nonviolence, peace will be longer, with less suffering and destruction.

The Buddha taught that a lasting peace can never be created by hatred, terror and war. Peace built upon aggression and oppression will not endure. As Aśoka, a great Buddhist emperor of ancient India, said: "Hatred does not cease by hatred, hatred ceases only by love." If we want to stop war, the Buddha says, we cannot use war; if we want to stop hatred, we cannot use hatred. The only way to end the vicious circle of hatred and killing is by using a more potent power, the power of love. It is through love, tolerance, mutual understanding

During a "Liberation of Life" ceremony, peace doves are released from Nirvāṇa Bridge, which joins the zendo and the monastery. Such ceremonies, where birds, animals and fish are set free, are common in all sects of Buddhism and symbolize the compassion that the Buddhas and Bodhisattvas have for all life forms.

and respect that we can overcome our enemies. By this method we transform our enemies into our friends. Buddhists believe that friends and enemies are created by our own behavior. The way to build up a peaceful world is through mutual respect between persons, communities and nations.

The hope of Buddhism is to develop a peaceful mind, a peaceful life and an awareness of relationships between oneself and others. Śākyamuni, by realizing the oneness of everything, of all living beings, taught this way: "I love the living beings as a mother loves her children." Whether the children are good or bad, the mother extends her love. Likewise with the Buddha. Whether living beings are good or not good, he extends universal love and compassion to all. According to Confucius, "All mankind in the four oceans are brothers." If we consider all mankind in the four oceans, or four directions—East and West, North and South—as our brothers, there is no reason to be angered by them or to fight with them. Confucian and Buddhist reasoning is similar to the Christian statement: "Love your enemies." It is a beautiful idea. Buddhism carries this idea one step further by not recognizing the existence of any enemy. There should be no distinctions made between friends and enemies, or between men and animals; rather love and compassion should be extended equally to all. This breakdown of dualistic thinking is a primary goal in Zen, as in other Buddhist sects. A common saying in Theravāda Buddhism is, "May all beings be well and happy." If one thinks in this manner, he cannot recognize any being as his enemy. If all mankind would apply this teaching to their lives, then the whole world would live in harmony.

Buddhist tradition also provides practical advice on how to build a better relationship between oneself and one's friends and how to eventually build a more peaceful, closer relationship between all men in society. The Buddha taught in the Sigāla Sūtra that certain disciplines should be practiced to cultivate friendship. Everyone has friends, and friends have duties to each other. As a true friend we ought: (1) to give our friends freedom; (2) to speak courteously to them; (3) to be helpful; (4) to be impartial; (5) to be sincere. Each individual has a different face, a different mind, a different thought, a different way of living. We must respect these differences. Although we may be able to speak our minds freely and candidly with our close friends, yet we should still treat them with as much respect and courtesy as we would extend to a stranger whom we have just met.

Friends should mutually help each other, particularly in times of trouble. Many people avoid their acquaintances who have some problem, but if we are a good friend, it is better to protect the friend and help him with his troubles. Friends are needed not only for the good times, but also for the bad. When a person's pursuits are failing and he is being dragged downward, he needs friends to bring him back up, to protect him, to give him refuge when he is in danger. As a good friend we ought: (1) to protect him when he is helpless; (2) to protect his property when he is unable to do so; (3) to become a refuge when he is in danger; (4) not to forsake him in his troubles; (5) to show consideration for his family. Fulfillment of these responsibilities not only aids the friend, but also helps us to grow in wisdom and compassion.

To help us to be aware of our responsibilities and to fufill them, we should practice meditation and apply it to daily life. Zen followers meditate because they wish to have self-realization, to rid themselves of pettiness and triviality, to make their lives simpler and richer. But self-realization is not only forgetting or not being bothered by external things, but also realizing relationships between oneself and others. Therefore, a person who practices Zen should keep in mind the reciprocation of four kindnesses that he is to fulfill. In the Sigāla Sūtra, the Buddha taught that each person is particularly indebted to four major forces in his life. Each man is profoundly affected by his culture, and much of his character and thought is formed by it. For this reason, he must fulfill his obligations to his country. It is obvious that the condition of the country profoundly affects the lives of its citizens. If the country is at peace, then the people share that peace. If the country is at war, they all share that tragedy. A practicing Buddhist must keep in mind his duties to the country in which he lives. He must help it to be a good and noble country.

As well, the Zen follower must respect his teacher. According to Confucius, a teacher is not only a man who educates a person intellectually and academically; he is also an example of virtuous life, of giving himself through love to his students. Thus, the student ought to honor his teacher since it is he who passes on the teachings toward growth and realization. Zen, particularly, emphasizes respect for the spiritual teachers who profoundly help the student on his quest for enlightenment.

A Buddhist has many duties to his parents. Nobody is born without parents. Everyone is indebted to his parents for life. A Vietnamese proverb states: "The tree has roots and the water has a stream." Therefore, children should remember their source and respect their parents. We must fulfill our filial piety, or our respect and love for our parents, because our parents loved us and supported us when we were young. Buddhism teaches that no matter how terrible parents may be, a child still owes his very life to them. Even if a parent should disown a child, the child should never forsake his parents. Should a student ask a Master, "Why must I respect my parents? They were unfit to raise children," he may reply: "Even if my mother were a thief, she would still be my mother." Sometimes people try to run from their families and forget their backgrounds, attempting to make a new life totally divorced from the old. Try as hard as he may, a man cannot escape his family, for it was that environment which shaped him. Even if a man leaves his family, his parents' blood still runs in his veins.

As mentioned earlier, everyone needs friends and should

respect them by performing certain duties. When we follow
these practices, we keep a better relationship between ourself,
members of our family and our friends. Having done this, we
keep a better relationship between ourselves and society. Then,
the highest and most extensive goal is to keep a better relationship with mankind. A Buddhist Bodhisattva should
consider that he is a part of the whole society—the society of
mankind. His ambition is to change this samsaric world into
Nirvāṇa. Nirvāṇa is a state of mind. If we are in a state of mind
of Nirvāṇa, then Nirvāṇa is here and now. If our mind is not
Nirvāṇa, then our world becomes the separate world of hatred
and anger which we call Saṃsāra. Therefore, the practicing
Bodhisattva tries at first to develop himself, then his relatives,
then members of society and mankind in order to change this
world into Nirvāṇa.

According to Western concepts, a man who wishes to go to
heaven must wait until after he dies. If he loved God and his
neighbors during his lifetime, then he may go to heaven. But
according to Buddhist thinking, Nirvāṇa can be discovered
here and now. In order to realize Nirvāṇa here and now, we
have to produce the Nirvāṇa Mind, here and now.

The meditation method of self-awareness, or Awareness
of the Wholeness and Awareness of the Oneness, is a technique to bring us to the realization of Nirvāṇa, here and
now. The person who gains true awareness of his self and
others, of his self and family, of his self and society, realizes that
all of us are parts which are related to the whole. If all of us
have a wonderful, peaceful mind, full of love and kindness,
then this mankind, this world, becomes love, kindness and
happiness.

While we must realize our oneness, the most important
teaching in Zen is self-realization and self-awareness. We must
realize that we have the capacity to become a Buddha, that we

have the capacity to become enlightened. Believing in that, we must never give up, but work diligently to build a better world for ourselves and others in this life, here and now.

In the eighteenth century Descartes said, "I think, therefore I am." Now, in the twentieth century, the author would like to change that famous dictum to "I am aware, therefore I am. I feel, therefore I am." Zen brings to us a different kind of feeling which teaches that there is no separation between oneself and others. All of us can become one. That is the new consciousness which is very necessary for man in the present as well as in the future. If man in ancient times sought awareness of some faraway supernatural being, and if man in modern times seeks awareness to improve all conditions of his life, then man in the future is not looking far away, is not looking down into material things, but is bringing us to a consciousness of ourselves. And that is most important.

When we have self-realization, at that time all of us and everything in this universe become one; there are no more differences between you and me, no more differences between East and West. Common sense makes this idea very difficult to understand. If we stand on the ground, we make the distinction of directions. But if we leave familiar ground and go higher, say up to the top of a mountain, and turn around several times, then every direction becomes the same—no East, no West, no North, no South. A person who practices religion is like a person who climbs to the top of a mountain. The many different methods are the many different ways one may climb the mountain. And many people follow different religions and climb different ways. But when the top of the mountain is reached, there is no longer different roads, no longer different paths. Only there! The top is there!

All of the different kinds of religion, of meditation, or of spiritual practice, are ways which bring to the superconsciousness a sense which is beyond discrimination, which is beyond commonsense differences. Everything is the same. In the movie "Illusion of Separateness," Baba Ram Dass states: "All different practices, including sitting meditation, are to bring us into the Gate." Into the Gate only. But then, what is that Gate? The Gate is the calmness of mind. Once we enter the Gate we see the world beyond. Through calmness of mind, through discipline of mind, we see what is beyond. Seeing beyond is very good. To experience Enlightenment or Nirvāṇa, first one has to reach the Gate. This task is something each person must do for himself. Only then can he see what is beyond, based on his own self-practice and self-discipline.

To explain about Nirvāṇa and enlightenment is like using a finger to point out the direction of the moon. If we wish to see the moon, we look at it, not at the finger. If we want to know Nirvāṇa and enlightenment we must find it out by ourselves, experience it for ourselves, rather than following what any Master explains.

According to Buddhism, everything as we perceive it is seen through the mind. The mind is like a window. Through the window we see the sky. The sky is neither square nor round, but because of the shape of the window we perceive it as being square or round. If we gaze on the sky with a peaceful mind, with a calm mind devoid of squareness or roundness, then the sky contains everything. In this way Zen brings us to non-discrimination. Through the practice of meditation, Zen brings to us eternity and peace.

Method of Practice

The meditator sits quietly and expands his ego-consciousness to a larger scale. He feels one with others and shares that feeling and happiness with others. That is the technique.

During the meditation period he holds nothing in his mind. When there is no ego-consciousness in the mind, at that moment he becomes one with others, aware of others. Now he sits quietly, forgetting everything, the past, the present, the future. He forgets the ego, expanding his consciousness to include everybody. He expands his ego-consciousness larger and larger and larger, joining all things together until all life becomes one. He and others are not different, but are one in the egoless consciousness. In the end there is no boundary, no expansion, because he and others are one. From this awareness of oneness, he develops feelings of universal love and compassion.

14

Words and Actions

When a person is hungry and wishes to eat, talking about food will not satisfy his hunger. Instead, he must prepare and cook actual food if he wishes to satiate his desire. Talking about Zen can never fulfill the hunger for the Zen experience. One must leave words behind and move directly to action. This need for direct experience is revealed in the following Zen poem.

> Consider the lives of birds and fish.
> Fish never weary of the water.
> But we do not know the true mind of fish
> For we are not a fish.
>
> Birds never tire of the wood.
> But we do not know the true mind of the bird
> For we are not a bird.

If we do not live Zen, we know nothing about it. Even if we study Zen philosophy extensively, if we do not practice it, we know very little about Zen. Intellectual understanding is second-hand knowledge; it is not direct experience. In order to have direct experience one must practice. Just as the student of calligraphy must hold the brush, dip it into ink and draw it across the paper, stroke by stroke, so must the Zen student practice his sitting meditation and apply it to his daily life. One can study Zen academically from a teacher, professor, or if fortunate enough, from a Master, or Roshi. One can study Zen by research, reading books about Zen or listening to the lectures of the Zen Masters. Nonetheless, the student of Zen must remember that intellectual understanding is not the heart of Zen. It is mere knowledge, indirect understanding; it is not an actual experience or true realization of Zen.

Language is very limited, while truth or reality is boundless. Thus, the limited tool of language cannot express the unlimited truth of reality. As Lao-tzu stated, "The Tao that can be talked about is not the Eternal Tao. The name that can be named is not the true name." Because reality or truth can never be adequately described, the Zen Master continually reminds his students that the teachings of the Master, even the teachings of the Buddha, are merely a finger to point out the moon. The finger is too short to reach the moon, and the finger is not the moon itself. If we wish to see the moon, it may be necessary to follow the direction of the finger, but eventually we must leave the finger there and directly see the moon ourselves. At that point we can then see what the moon actually is.

When Śākyamuni Buddha was alive, many disciples gathered about him. Of the 1250 *bhikkhu*s, *bhikkhunī*s, Arhats and Bodhisattvas, two disciples were especially close to the Buddha, Ven. Mahākāśyapa and Ven. Ānanda. Ānanda was intellectual, brilliant, knowledgeable; Mahākāśyapa was advanced in meditation, in practice. When it came time to choose his successor, the Buddha chose Mahākāśyapa. Hung-Jen, the Fifth Patriarch of Zen in China, had five hundred devotees who studied under him in his monastery. The head monk was Shen-Hsiu, intellectual, brilliant, knowledgeable. But Hung-Jen named Hui-

Neng, an illiterate kitchen monk, as his successor. Hui-Neng was named as the Sixth Patriarch, not for his education, his intellectual knowledge or study. Rather, he was selected because his practice revealed that his realization was beyond words and language.

Because language and intellectual knowledge are indirect tools, they are not the heart of Zen. Zen is founded upon the historical moment of the raising of the flower by Śākyamuni Buddha and the smile of comprehension of Mahākāśyapa. Its later development was in the special message that Bodhidharma, the twenty-eighth Patriarch brought from India to China:

> A special transmission outside the scriptures;
> No dependence upon words and letters;
> Direct pointing at the mind of man;
> Seeing into one's nature and the attainment of Buddhahood.

Bodhidharma taught that the writings of the various Masters and Patriarchs, even the teachings of the Buddha, are expedient tools. Thus, one should not depend upon them solely nor cling to them. The more important method of teaching in Zen is direct experience, direct looking into oneself to discover the Buddha nature and attain Buddhahood. In other words, not outward but inward search is the core of Zen teaching.

Reading many Zen books may provide the groundwork for the understanding of Zen, but knowledge and wisdom are not the same. Knowledge is gained by learning from external sources, while wisdom is developed within from inner experience and realization. In Zen, wisdom is the more important, and it is gained through practice and insight. The practice of Zen is not limited to sitting. We can sit for only a part of the twenty-four hours in a day. It is difficult for us to sit constantly unless we are participating in a special training period or *sesshin*.

Therefore, the practical Chinese and Japanese prolong the meditation period by applying the techniques of Zen to daily life and its activities. During gardening there is zazen. In painting, tea ceremony, reading, studying, there is zazen. Zazen may be washing dishes, cooking food, carrying water. In all daily activities, still zazen is there.

Hui-Neng practiced zazen totally in his daily life. He had no time to sit in meditation, for he was busy cooking food, carrying water and washing dishes for his five hundred friends in the monastery. However, during all his manual labor he practiced disciplining his mind, controlling his mind, until he attained Oneness of mind and body, subject and object, himself and the universe. His deep realization from the practice of mindfulness was accepted by the Fifth Patriarch, Hung-Jen, who presented him with the patriarchal bowl and robe, as symbols of his succession and authority.

A question frequently asked by the student of Zen is, "If knowledge is not important, then why is there verbal teaching at all? If nothing is good or bad, wrong or right, why follow moral codes?" In answer to these questions, we must remember that true Zen cannot be practiced if the student does not follow the teachings of the Buddha and the Masters. Śākyamuni Buddha taught that in order to obtain perfect enlightenment one must develop two qualities: *prajñā,* or wisdom, depicted by Mañjuśrī, who holds the sword of wisdom to cut off all delusions, and *karuṇā,* or compassion, represented by Kwan-Yin (Avalokiteśvara), holding the sacred healing waters to comfort the suffering. To develop wisdom in order to destroy ignorance and illusion, one should begin with observance of the precepts (*śīla*) and practice meditation (*samādhi*). To develop compassion in order to love and help others, one should practice the six *pāramitā*s of *dāna* (generosity), *śīla* (morality), *kṣānti* (patience), *vīrya* (energy), *dhyāna* (meditation) and

prajñā (wisdom). Of the six *pāramitā*s the foundation stone is
dāna, giving selflessly. In giving one should make his loving-
kindness available to others both materially and spiritually.

The Buddha taught that the heart of Buddhist practice is
caring about all sentient beings. Mahāyāna Buddhism, to
which Zen belongs, particularly stresses this concern for all life
forms. Buddha himself is an example of this practice. At the
time of his enlightenment he could have entered Nirvāṇa, but
he determined, instead, to remain in the samsaric world to
guide others to experience enlightenment for themselves. The
fundamentals of Buddhist practice, in both Theravāda and
Mahāyāna tradition, can be divided into three major classifica-
tions: (1) not to commit evil; (2) to cultivate what is good;
(3) to purify the mind. Purifying the mind is most important
and can be easily attended to during sitting meditation, but the
first two goals—not to commit evil and to cultivate what is
good—are not easily practiced in our daily life. They take great
concentration and selflessness. To remind disciples of these
principles, in many Zen monasteries a *gāthā* is chanted before
meals: "In accepting this meal, I vow to abstain from all evil, to
cultivate all good and to benefit all sentient beings." The
person who practices Zen and hopes to have an experience of
enlightenment and Nirvāṇa should not commit evil. Zen
Masters may say: "According to the truth, according to the
absolute, nothing is good, nothing is bad; nothing wrong,
nothing right." In spite of what the Master says, no one will ever
see him commit evil. It is only after one transcends his limited
mind and reaches full consciousness, or enlightenment, that
one does not have to be concerned with good and evil. For a
perfected being such as the Buddha will never create evil.

The first concern in becoming a perfect being is to refrain
from committing evil. At the same time, one must cultivate
and practice all good, good for himself and for others. Zen

emphasizes the oneness and harmony of life. When all beings live in oneness and harmony, helping each other, there will be no discrimination between self and others, no differentiation between giver and receiver. From the Buddhist point of view none of us is separate. We are all parts of each other. The attained Master sees no distinction between himself and others; he does not cling to the concept of subject and object. Therefore, a person who truly practices Zen cannot walk away from suffering. He is ready to share not only the happiness, but also the sorrow of other persons. Because of the emphasis on oneness between oneself and others, the Mahāyāna Buddhist never can attain Nirvāṇa if others are still suffering.

Jizō Bodhisattva made the vow that as long as one being still suffers in hell he will not enter Nirvāṇa. He will re-enter the hells again and again to help any being caught in the sorrows of Saṃsāra. Likewise, Kwan-Yin Bodhisattva also remains in the world of Saṃsāra to help all sentient beings in their troubles and sufferings. She is depicted standing on a lotus flower. As the lotus rises from the dirt and mud, it offers beautiful color and perfume. Kwan-Yin Bodhisattva is always present in the ocean of suffering to save all beings.

In China, Japan and Vietnam, many Buddhist temples and Zen monasteries place a Kwan-Yin statue on the altar and a Jizō image in the garden. These shrines remind followers that in order to develop themselves to perfect enlightenment, they must practice loving-kindness and act with compassion in daily life. Without that action, one never can experience perfect enlightenment. Hakuin Zenji, a great Zen Master of Japan, said in his "Song of Zazen,"

> Sentient beings are primarily all Buddhas.
> It is like ice and water;
> Apart from the water, no ice can exist.
> Outside sentient beings, where is the Buddha found?

In order to develop the Bodhisattva qualities, the Zen adept must always be mindful to discipline his three karmas: body action, mouth action and mind action. As we sit in meditation we have very good behavior, but if we do not discipline the mind, when we get up from the zafu and leave the zendo, we may act badly. Therefore, we must maintain mindfulness not only to sit in perfect posture, but also to maintain perfect action and perfect speech in our daily lives. As we sit in meditation, the mind is quiet, and we control our mouths. But when we get up from the zafu and leave the zendo, it is easy to criticize others or to say something which will cause others pain and hurt. We must discipline the mouth and control our speech as well as develop meditation and wisdom. A Chinese proverb states it this way, "One word spoken, four strong horses cannot pull it back." Before we speak anything, we must consider the result, whether or not it is beneficial to ourselves and others. If what we say harms ourselves and hurts others, it is best to refrain from speech. It is recorded in the *Dhammapada* that the Buddha said, "Let not one seek others' faults, things left done and undone by others, but one's own deeds done and undone."

When a person practices loving-kindness and compassion, he thinks well of other people, and his words and actions reflect this kindness. All action and all speech come from the mind and thought. If the mind does not think kindly, it is difficult to have kind speech and action. A Buddhist tries his utmost to be mindful of his thought, sometimes called "watching the thoughts," because he knows that thought is the foundation of all action and speech.

Sitting meditation is a technique for disciplining and purifying the mind. When the mind is purified, *satori,* or enlightenment, is not far away. Dogen Zenji, founder of the Soto Zen School in Japan, said that "Zazen and *satori* are one." That is, sitting in meditation and enlightenment are one. While one sits, his body does not commit evil, and his mouth does not speak evil. The mind is also very calm, quiet and pure. Thus, sitting meditation is a period of enlightenment, or at least the cause or preparation for enlightenment. However, since the zazen period is relatively short, the disciplined mind obtained from zazen must be carried into everyday life. That purified mind must be transformed into action. Every day becomes a day of practice.

The Zen student experiences every day and appreciates the beauty of every season. If a person limits his mind, he cannot appreciate the totality of life. To practice Zen is not only to enjoy life during its blissful or ecstatic moments, but also to be content during its tragedies and sorrows. Usually we are happy when life runs smoothly and peacefully, but when there arises some trouble or difficulty, we feel distressed and uncomfortable. In actuality there is nothing so terrible. There can never be success without failure, so we should not worry about our failures. Success and failure, disappointment and satisfaction, all depend on the mind. Why should we worry or be so serious about things. We must take it easy and relax. Everything comes and goes, nothing should bother us too much.

The same is true of Zen practice. If we sit a little longer than usual, a small backache may develop or a leg fall asleep, but we should not be concerned about these things or allow them to bother us. Later, after we move a little and stand up for a while, everything is fine. During sitting meditation the mind may wander, the subconscious revelations may be frightening or very intense, the emotions overpowering, yet continued practice puts an end to these problems. Sometimes there is a good lesson to be learned in a little difficulty. We learn more from failure than success, for failure provides valuable experience in life. Pictures of Bodhidharma frequently carry four Chinese characters which mean, "Fall down seven times, stand up the eighth." The importance of life is not measured by how many successes there are, but how many crises are resolved.

Since life is a long journey, especially the journey from Saṃsāra to Nirvāṇa, from ignorance to enlightenment, patience is required. The third of the six *pāramitā*s of Bodhisattva practice is patience. The desire for realization, for enlightenment, for saving all sentient beings requires great patience. One must move straight ahead, diligently working to accomplish his goal. Confucius teaches, "Do not wish for quick results, nor look for small advantages. If one seeks quick results, he will not attain the ultimate goal. If he is led astray by small advantages, he will never accomplish great things." It is the same for the person who practices Zen and wishes to fulfill his Bodhisattva vows. The effort is most important. There are so many problems that they cannot all be solved, but one must do his best each day to solve what he can. Perhaps, there are many obstacles and difficulties, but one can overcome them one by one. Nothing should be left for tomorrow that can be done today. Each day the Zen student must do his best to fulfill that day. Then he should let the day pass, not clinging, not attached, not worried about anything; he must let the mind be free. If there is something that cannot be accomplished today, then it cannot be done today. Why should we be bothered and worried? There will be time later to do it. Tomorrow will come—many tomorrows.

In the tradition of Zen Buddhism, before each sitting, ceremony or religious activity is completed, the four Bodhisattva vows are chanted. One of them states: "Sentient beings are innumerable, I vow to save them all." With millions of beings in this universe as well as in other universe systems, how can we save them all? It is impossible. Nevertheless, we can help whoever and whenever we can; also we can extend our love, kindness and good thoughts to all living beings, whether

we can save them or not. There are people who think that they
are too poor to give; others want to help, but think they do
not have enough energy or skillful means. These thoughts
are not correct. Anyone, in any condition, still has something
to give—materially, emotionally or spiritually. Anyone can
smile or have kind, sympathetic thoughts, which can be extended to others to comfort them. No one is too poor to give,
and no one is too weak to act. With a strong will and firm
determination, a man can do anything he wants, including
saving all sentient beings.

One of the most famous sayings of Zen Buddhism is,
"Nirvāṇa is Saṃsāra; Saṃsāra is Nirvāṇa." How can we change
Saṃsāra to Nirvāṇa? First we must cleanse the mind, speech
and actions. Secondly, we must guide others to the truth—help
all living beings to self-realization, to enlightenment. Then
Nirvāṇa is possible here and now. It is not so far away. To
attain Nirvāṇa all we need is practice and action. From practice
and action we will transcend our limited mind and reach the
enlightened mind. From that state of mind we will experience
Nirvāṇa here in this world of Saṃsāra in the present moment.
Now there are no words—only action, only Nirvāṇa.

Method of Practice

Mahāyāna Buddhism requires that the enlightened ones
and those advanced along the path show the way to others.
However, beginners also can help other beings in this world.
Mahāyāna Buddhist tradition emphasizes that each person who
practices Buddhism should see himself as holding a candle in
his hand. The candle will help him to see the way, and others
may also benefit from the light. For that reason Mahāyāna
Buddhists do not wait until perfect enlightenment before they
act; they begin to act when they begin to practice. Therefore,

the Four Great Bodhisattva vows are recited daily in Buddhist temples, monasteries and Zen centers at the close of services and meditation. If the reader will recite them following his daily meditation and practice them in his daily life, they will encourage him in his studies and spur him on in his efforts to obtain enlightenment and Nirvāṇa. These great vows express the infinite compassion of the Buddhas, and in chanting them we express our desire to become as the great Bodhisattvas and Buddhas, a person who is willing both to improve himself and to share his happiness and his enlightenment with others.

Four Great Bodhisattva Vows

Sentient beings are innumerable,
    I vow to save them all.
The deluding passions are inexhaustible,
    I vow to destroy them all.
The gates of the Dharma are immeasurable,
    I vow to enter them all.
The Buddha-Way is supreme,
    I vow to attain it.

Appendix A

The Matter
of Soul in Buddhism

The rebecoming or rebirth doctrine in Buddhism has been narrowly understood. When almost everyone hears the word "rebirth," they conceive of it as involving the continuation of a permanent soul in a succession of physical bodies. It is thought that, according to this doctrine, when one dies, the soul will leave the body, wander in space and enter a new-born body, or go to a heaven or a hell for a certain time before becoming reborn in a human or animal body.

However, Buddhism holds that after a man dies, there is nothing at all which leaves one body and enters another. As we know, Buddhism teaches that the individual is the continuous combination of five *skandhas*, which include all the physiological and psychological elements (*rūpa*—physical form, *vedanā*—sensations, *saṃjñā*—conceptions, *saṃskāra*—mental formations, *vijñāna*—consciousness). The first, *rūpa,* is the physical constituent, and the other four are the mental (spiritual) components. All of these mental components can only be manifested when there is a basis-organ for their arising, and this basis-organ is the physical body, or the physiological components of the individual. Thus, the physical body in Buddhism is called the "body-organ." If the body-organ is dead, all the mental processes can no longer function, but return to the subconsciousness and are deposited there in the form of seeds.

Just as the physical body, the combination of the four major elements (solidity—earth, fluidity—water, air—wind and heat—fire), undergoes a perpetual transformation, so the four mental components form a continuous and incessantly changing current. The body is forever changing every moment: from one moment to the next it is not the same. The mental current proceeds in the same way. Every moment there is a new feeling and a new perception arising to replace the old which has faded away, or has sunk into the deep recesses of memory, returning to the seed. Because it is always changing, that mental current is not an eternally identical unit; therefore, we cannot call it a "self" or "ego." A thing that we can label as a soul must be an identical, unchanging self controlling our body. Here Buddhism holds that there is no self: this means that there is no soul. The mental components of man are only the mental components. They arise and function when the appropriate conditions are present (i.e., active body basis-organ) and return to the state of seeds in the subconsciousness when the physical elements are destroyed (i.e., with the death of the physical body).

Many people believe that behind the psychological and physical elements, which are always changing, there must be an element which is unchanging. That element is itself the soul, and that element recognizes itself as an ego. If there were no soul, it is asked, how can we explain the identical character which exists throughout change, the identical character which everybody feels exists in oneself and in others?

However, if we examine this issue with care, we will discover that the explanation of identical character does not necessarily require the existence of any ego, or soul.

Several years ago I bought a bicycle. This year that bicycle is much older. I have replaced many parts of it at different times, including the parts of the body, but I still have the feeling that the bicycle is the one I bought several years ago. So, on what grounds can I discover the identical character of the bicycle in its process of evolution? Perhaps because that bicycle contains within itself an "unchanging element," a "soul"? If it were this way, then what should we call the unchanging element? Should we call it the soul of the bicycle or the ego of the bicycle? The soul of the bicycle cannot be found because there is no unchanging element, no soul, no ego. There is only the mental and physical phenomena, which are always changing.

On what ground do we base the notion of the identical character of a thing. According to Buddhism, we feel that there is something identical persisting through the changing phenomena because we are subject to erroneous ideas. These erroneous ideas are illusions imposed upon the continuously changing nature of phenomena.

All phenomena are perpetually subject to transformation, to arising and cessation at every moment. From the seed comes the manifestation, the manifestation returns to the seed, and in this transformation, arising and cessation happen so rapidly that we feel that there is an identical character of a single thing persisting through the incessant change. When we twirl a speck of fire at the end of a stick, we see a "circle of fire," but in fact, that circle is only a continuous illusion which is comprised of many specks of fire, always changing.

I say "many specks of fire, always changing," give rise to that circle because there is not one speck of fire, but countless specks of fire. Since fire is merely a process of energy transformation, as it moves down the stick, consuming it, the fire constantly changes. The last speck of fire is not the same as the previous speck of fire. Therefore, the speck of fire on the top of the circle is not the same as the speck of fire at the bottom of the circle. However, the last speck of fire is not completely different from the preceding speck of fire, because if there were no preceding speck of fire, there would be no later speck of fire. It is this continuous current that gives us the erroneous idea of an identical character. This issue is elucidated for us by a passage in *The Questions of King Milinda,* a dialogue between the Venerable Nāgasena and the King Milinda:

> Suppose a man, O king, were to light a lamp, would it burn the night through?
>
> Yes, it might do so.
>
> Now is it the same flame which burns in the first watch of the night, Sir, and in the second?
>
> No.
>
> Or the same that burns in the second watch and in the third?
>
> No.
>
> Then is there one lamp in the first watch, and another in the second, and another in the third?
>
> No. The light comes from the same lamp all the night through.
>
> In exactly the same way, O king, do the elements of being join one another in serial succession: one element arises, another perishes, and another arises, succeeding each other, as it were, instantaneously. Therefore, neither as the same nor as a different person do you arrive at your latest aggregation of consciousness.

We can compare our physical body with the lamp, wick and oil, and our mental structure with the incessantly changing flame: there is not an "identical unit," but neither are there differences. ("There is no one, there are no differences" – *The Awakening of Faith.*) Our psycho-physical organism is not an identical unchanging unit, but rather a continuously changing current. The seemingly identical character of things and of our psycho-physical organism is only an illusion.

If there is no such entity as an unchanging ego, a soul, what is reborn? What becomes? What is the subject of the current of birth and death? This question has tormented many people. We often see in Buddhist sutras stories of rebirth in which, for example, a man in Benares dies and is reborn as an animal in Kapilavastu. So what leaves the body of that man and enters the body of the animal? How does the death of one living being connect with the birth of another?

As we know, Buddhism does not recognize the existence of a transmigrating soul. Buddhism only holds to cause and effect, or conditioned co-production (Pratītyasamutpāda): any result or effect must have a previous cause. As long as craving exists, the life will continue to exist. As long as craving exists, all the seeds in the store-consciousness (*ālaya-vijñāna*) still bear the tendencies of rebirth, which means the tendencies for the arising of birth and death. If, with the end of life, all the craving is destroyed and ignorance no longer exists, then all the seeds become transformed into wisdom, the store-consciousness returns to the fundamentally enlightened Essence, and the current of birth and death no longer continues. But if craving still exists, the store-consciousness sinks into the state of impurity and cannot yet attain liberation from birth and death. Therefore, the current of life must continue.

In *The Dharma of Buddha*, the Ven. Jagdish Kasyapa explains the Buddhist view of rebirth by an analogy. Everyone knows of the Hundred Years War between France and England. To say "Hundred Years War" means that many battles were fought over a time span of one hundred years. All the battles occurred at different times and at different places and with different weapons. But why do all the battles appear together as a single entity, a "Hundred Years War"? Why didn't the fighting stop after the first battle, so that later battles could not take place? Perhaps because the hatred between the two countries still continued. That idea of hate was the cause of war and also was the cause for the continuation of the sequence of battles. As long as that idea existed, the battles had the condition to exist. In the same way, as long as craving exists, the current of birth and death exists with a new body, new circumstances and a new world.

A wave appears here. Why? Because of the impulse of the wave over there. This wave rises and subsides, and when it subsides, it originates a new impulse. By the force of this impulse, there arises over there a new wave: that new wave is the result of this wave. In the same way, the sequence of lives in the past originate the causal karma which conditions the life in the present, and the causal karma originating in the present life conditions the sequence of lives in the future. All of our causal karma—that of thought, word and action, as well as our sense impressions—forever returns to and sinks into the store-consciousness; thus, nothing is ever lost. All these comprise the karmic factors which propel us into a new life.

The Buddhist doctrine of non-self, or non-soul, is very complex, and much more could be written about it than is contained herein. We must, however, for the present remain content with what has been said.

Appendix B

The Song of Zazen

by Hakuin Zenji

Sentient beings are primarily all Buddhas:
It is like ice and water,
Apart from water no ice can exist;
Outside sentient beings, where do we find the Buddhas?

Not knowing how near the Truth is,
We seek it far away—what a pity!
We are like him who, in the midst of water,
Cries in thirst so imploringly;
We are like the son of a rich man
Who wandered away among the poor.

The reason why we transmigrate through the six worlds
Is because we are lost in the darkness of ignorance;
Going astray further and further in the darkness,
When are we able to be free from birth-and-death?

As for Zazen practice in the Mahāyāna,
We have no words to praise it fully:
The virtues of perfection such as charity, morality,
And the invocation of the Buddha's name, confession, and
    ascetic discipline,
And many other good deeds of merit—
All these issue from the practice of Zazen.
Even those who have practiced it for just one sitting
Will see all their evil karma erased;
Nowhere will they find evil paths,
But the Pure Land will be near at hand.

With a reverential heart, if we listen to this Truth even once,
And praise it, and gladly embrace it,
We will surely be blessed most infinitely.
But, if we concentrate within
And testify to the truth that Self-Nature is no-nature,
We have really gone beyond foolish talk.

The gate of the oneness of cause and effect is opened;
The path of non-duality and non-trinity runs straight ahead.
To regard the form of no-form as form,
Whether going or returning, we cannot be any place else;
To regard the thought of no-thought as thought;
Whether singing or dancing, we are the voice of the Dharma.

How boundless the cleared sky of Samādhi!
How transparent the perfect moonlight of the
    Fourfold Wisdom!

At this moment what more need we seek?
As the Truth eternally reveals itself,
This very place is the Lotus Land of Purity,
This very body is the Body of the Buddha.

Glossary

(All terms are Sanskrit unless otherwise indicated.)

Amita (*Amitābha*): The Buddha of Infinite Light and Infinite Life, the presiding Buddha of the Western Paradise worshipped in Pure Land Buddhism.

Ānanda: A close disciple of Śākyamuni Buddha; the Third Patriarch.

Anātma (*Anatta*, Pali): Non-self, no-soul, as opposed to *ātman*, a basic tenet of Hinduism, rejected by the Buddha.

Anitya (*Anicca*, Pali): Impermanence, the ever changing nature of all phenomena.

Arhat: Saint of Theravāda Buddhism; freed from all desires and defilements, freed from craving and rebirth, perfected being.

Aśoka: A Buddhist emperor of ancient India.

Ātman: Soul, non-changing quality; a basic tenet of Hinduism, which was rejected by the Buddha.

Avalokiteśvara: The Bodhisattva of Universal Compassion.

Avidyā: Ignorance, misconception, the state of the unenlightened mind.

Bhikṣu (Bhikkhu, Pali): Beggar, mendicant, Buddhist monk; one who follows the 250 precepts of the Buddhist Saṅgha.

Bhikṣuṇī (Bhikkhunī, Pali): Female mendicant, Buddhist nun; one who follows the Saṅgha's 348 precepts for nuns.

Bīja: Seed; in Buddhism *bīja* refers to karmic residues in the *ālaya-vijñāna* (store-house consciousness).

Bodhi: Enlightenment.

Bodhidharma: The Twenty-eighth Indian Patriarch and First Chinese Patriarch who brought Zen Buddhism to China in the early 6th century.

Bodhisattva: A follower of Mahāyāna Buddhism who is enlightened, but who stays in the cycle of birth and death in order to work for the enlightenment and salvation of all sentient beings.

Buddha: The Enlightened One; the historical founder of Buddhism; anyone who has achieved Perfect Enlightenment.

Buddhadharma: The teaching of the Buddha.

Ch'an: The Chinese word for Zen, q.v.

Chuang Tzu: A Taoist sage, 3rd century B.C.

Chūdō (Jap.): The Middle Path of Buddhism.

Confucius: Chinese sage, 6th century B.C., whose philosophy stressed ethics, moral laws and obligations.

Dāna: Giving, charity; the presentation of alms to monks and nuns.

Dhāraṇī: A verse of mystical syllables; abbreviation of a sutra to its essential elements.

Dharma: Law, doctrine or truth; the timeless law of enlightenment; the teaching of the Buddha as the fullest expression of that law.

Dharmakāya: The Absolute Body of the Buddha; the unconditioned reality considered as the true nature of a Buddha.

Dhyāna: Meditation; a state of absorption resulting from the practice of meditation.

Dogen Zenji: The Japanese Zen master who introduced Soto Zen Buddhism into Japan, 11th century A.D.

Duḥkha: Suffering, pain, sorrow, discontent; the state of the world of Saṃsāra.

Gāthā: A stanza or poem expressing some Buddhist concept.

Hīnayāna: The "Little Vehicle," the more conservative school of Buddhism which prevails in Southeast Asia. See also Theravāda.

Hui-Ke: The disciple of Bodhidharma who became the Second Chinese Patriarch of Zen Buddhism.

Hui-Neng: The Sixth Patriarch of Zen Buddhism in China (died 713 A.D.).

Hung-Jen: The Fifth Patriarch of Zen Buddhism in China (died 675 A.D.).

Jizō Bosatsu: The Japanese name for Kṣitigarbha Bodhisattva.

Joriki (Jap.): Concentration-power, one of the three goals of Zen meditation.

Kalpa: Aeon, billions of years; repeated cycles of creation and decay of a universe; A small Kalpa is the time it takes for a man's life to decrease one year every 100 years from 840,000 to ten and to increase in the same way from ten to 840,000. Twenty small Kalpas make a medium Kalpa, and four medium Kalpas made a large Kalpa.

Karma: Volitional actions as causes bringing future retribution; the moral law of cause and effect.

Karuṇā: Compassion, universal love; one of the two perfections needed for the attainment of Buddhahood.

Keisaku (Jap.): Awakening stick; slender, flat wooden paddle used to strike students on shoulder or back to relieve tension and reduce fatigue during zazen. The sound of its slap is supposed to awaken the disciple to *satori*.

Kensho: The Japanese term for seeing into one's true nature, the first flash of enlightenment or *satori*.

Kinhin: (Jap.): Walking meditation.

Koan (Jap.): A puzzling philosophical problem used as a topic in Zen meditation, emphasized especially in Rinzai Zen.

Kṣitigarbha: A compassionate Bodhisattva who has vowed to remain in hell in order to enlighten the beings there.

Kwan-Yin: The Chinese name for the Bodhisattva Avalokiteśvara, q.v.

Lao-Tzu: Old Man, Chinese Sage, 7th century B.C., whose philosophy emphasized harmony with nature.

Mahākāśyapa: The Second Indian Patriarch of Buddhism who inherited the transmission from the Buddha.

Mahāprajñāpāramitā Sūtra: "Great Wisdom Practice for Crossing to the Shore of Nirvāṇa Sūtra", collection of sixteen sutras, including the *Heart Sūtra, Diamond Sūtra* and *Perfection of Wisdom Sūtra*.

Mahāyāna: The "Great Vehicle," the progressive and comprehensive form of Buddhism which prevails in Northern and Far Eastern Asia.

Manas: Intellect, part of the mind that thinks, source of all discrimination; ego-consciousness.

Mañjuśrī Bodhisattva: The attendant to the left of Śākyamuni Buddha; the personification of the wisdom of the Buddha.

Mokkyō (Jap.): A wooden percussion instrument used in chanting.

Mondo (Jap.): Formal question and answer session between Master and student in the Rinzai Zen school. The Master uses *mondo* to help awaken the adept to his true nature.

Mu: The Japanese term for "nothingness," signifying the Buddhist doctrine that all things are nothingness. See *Śūnyatā.*

Mujodo-No-Taigen (Jap.): "The actualization of the Supreme Way"; the fusing of the truth realized in enlightenment with one's everyday life.

Nirvāṇa: The extinction of birth-and-death; the highest state of bliss, peace and purity; the unconditioned reality.

Obaku Zen: The school of Zen Buddhism in Japan that combines formal Zen meditation with devotion to Amita Buddha.

Pāramitā: Crossing from Saṃsāra to Nirvāṇa; practice which leads to Nirvāṇa; the six practices of the Bodhisattva who has attained the enlightened mind: charity, morality, patience, energy, meditation and wisdom.

Parinirvāṇa: The stage of final Nirvāṇa achieved by an enlightened being at the time of physical death.

Pi-Kuan (Chinese): "Wall-contemplation," the practice of Zen meditation while facing a blank wall.

Prajñā: Wisdom, one of the two perfections required for Buddhahood.

Rinzai Zen: The school of Zen Buddhism named after the Chinese Zen master Rin-zai (Lin-Chi).

Roshi: The formal Japanese title for a Zen master.

Rūpa: Physical form, body, matter.

Śākyamuni: The "Silent Sage of the Sakya clan," name of the present Buddha.

Samādhi: The state of mental concentration resulting from the practice of meditation.

Saṃsāra: The ocean of birth and death; the wheel of becoming; the phenomenal universe.

Saṅgha: The Buddhist monastic order.

Sanzen (Jap.): An interview with a Zen master to receive guidance in meditation.

Satori (Jap.): The Japanese Zen term for enlightenment.

Sensei (Jap.): Teacher.

Sesshin (Jap.): Special periods of intensive meditation practice in Zen Buddhism lasting from a few days to a few months.

Shen-Hsiu: A disciple of the Fifth Patriarch Hung-Jen who lost the patriarchship to Hui-Neng.

Shikan-Taza (Jap.): "Just sitting," a type of meditation used in Soto Zen which involves sitting with a mind empty of all thoughts.

Shinku-Myou (Jap.): "True Emptiness, Wonderful Existence," a philosophical description of the ultimate reality.

Śīla: Moral discipline, the observance of precepts.

Skandha: Aggregates of conditioned phenomena. There are five: the first is *rūpa,* physical matter, and the last four are *nāma,* mind functions.

Soto Zen: The school of Zen Buddhism originating in China and introduced into Japan by Dogen Zenji.

Śrāmaṇera (*Śrāmaṇerika,* fem.): A monk, nun, one who has taken the first ten precepts of the Saṅgha.

Śūnyatā: Emptiness; the Buddhist doctrine that all conditioned things as well as the Absolute are empty of a determinate nature.

Sūtra: Buddhist scripture; words spoken by the Buddha.

Suzuki, D. T.: A famous Japanese Zen Buddhist scholar (1870–1966).

Tao Te Ching: A record of the Taoist philosophy of Lao-Tzu.

Tathāgata: "One who has gone thus"; the Buddha, an Enlightened One.

Tathatā: "Suchness," a philosophical term for the ultimate reality.

Theravāda: "Doctrine of the Elders," the school of Buddhism which flourishes in Southeast Asia.

Ullumbāna (Bon, Jap.): Filial Piety Day.

Un-Shui: "Clouds and water," a Japanese term for a Buddhist monk.

Van-Hanh: A great Vietnamese Zen master, 11th century A.D.

Vedanā: Feelings, sensations.

Wu-Ti: The emperor of China when Bodhidharma arrived from the West.

Yin-Yang: The polar opposites of Taoist thought, e.g., light and dark, male and female, etc.

Zabuton (Jap.): A thick mat placed under a meditation pillow to ease long periods of sitting meditation.

Zafu (Jap.): A round meditation pillow, approximately 15″ diameter and 4–6″ thick.

Zazen (Jap.): Sitting meditation.

Zen (Jap.): The school of Mahāyāna Buddhism which emphasizes meditation as a means to enlightenment; the practice of meditation.

Zendo (Jap.): A meditation hall.